CAMPING GUIDE TO TASMANIA

Craig Lewis and Cathy Savage

BOILING BILLY PUBLICATIONS

www.boilingbilly.net.au

www.woodslane.com.au

Boiling Billy, a licenced imprint of
Woodslane Press
10 Apollo Street
Warriewood NSW 2102 Australia
Email: info@woodslane.com.au
Tel: 02 8445 2300
www.woodslane.com.au

This fully revised and updated 5th edition 2018

ISBN: 9781921874314

Printed in China by Asia Pacific Offset

Please be aware that conditions constantly change. Campsites are subject to closure without notice and camping fees may rise. It is the responsibility of individuals to enquire about the status of areas they wish to visit prior to departure.

NATIONAL LIBRARY OF AUSTRALIA

A catalogue record for this book is available from the National Library of Australia

Your Help Please

Boiling Billy Publications welcomes feedback from readers. If you find things are different than what is stated in this guide, or you know of a suitable campsite that we can update in subsequent editions, then please write or e-mail us at

Boiling Billy Publications
Nimmitabel NSW 2631
Tel: 02 6454 6162
E-mail: info@boilingbilly.com.au
Web: www.boilingbilly.com.au
www.facebook.com/boilingbilly

Like

MIX
Paper from responsible sources
FSC® C012521
FSC www.fsc.org

ABOUT THE AUTHORS

Craig Lewis and Cathy Savage have travelled extensively throughout Australia over the last 20 or so years, visiting some of the very best camping destinations secreted away across this vast country.

The pair reckon that the wide open spaces of the Australian outdoors is a great place to be, so after intermittent stints of travelling between work commitments, they began submitting magazine and newspaper travel articles to help fund their adventures. Before long they moved into authoring books and in 1995 established Boiling Billy Publications to write and publish accurate and up-to-date guidebooks for people who, like themselves, love travelling and exploring Australia's great outdoors.

As part of their ongoing field research schedule, they generally camp out around 100 nights each year in various campsites from the coast to the deserts. Tasmania remains one of their favourite states for going camping.

When not on the road travelling their home base is on a secluded farm, tucked away high up on the coastal escarpment in the Monaro region of South-East New South Wales, looking out over the Brogo Wilderness in Wadbilliga National Park.

Craig and Cathy's website is at www.boilingbilly.com.au

Contents

Dove Lake Boatshed, Cradle Mountain

Regional Map of Tasmania

REGIONAL MAPS LEGEND

HOBART	Capital City
Launceston	Town Major
Maydena	Town
Tasman Highway	Road Name
	Freeway
	Principal Road
	Secondary Road
	Railway
	River
	State Border
	Waterbody

MAP REGIONS

How to use this Guide

Camping Guide to Tasmania is designed in an easy to use format that makes finding that perfect campsite simple. The guide has been broken into five different chapters covering the major tourism regions throughout Tasmania.

In this book, each park, forest or reserve throughout the state that allows camping has its own entry. You can locate their approximate positions on the regional maps at the beginning of each chapter. These maps provide an overview of the region covered in the chapter and provide a starting reference point. There are also a number of more detailed maps for some of the national parks, forests and reserves throughout the guide. The grey boxes on the regional maps at the start of each region show the area covered by these maps in that region.

Each entry, whether it be a national park, forest reserve or riverside area, has detailed information relating to that site including access details, map references (MR) and some include GPS coordinates. These map references refer to the Touring Maps section and are useful for locating the campsite. For example, MR: Map 8 J4 refers to Touring Map 8 and the grid reference is J4 – this is the location of River and Rocks camping area in Moulting Lagoon Game Reserve.

We use symbols to detail the facilities and activities at each site.

We also include Further Information boxes for the authority to contact for making enquiries or bookings, along with prices and other details that apply to the camping site.

Although all care has been taken when compiling this guide and is correct at the time of going to print, note that conditions at campsites are constantly changing. Camping fees may be introduced to previously free areas or may be increased from what is listed. Some areas may also be closed from time to time – fire and flood, for example, can have a marked affect on an area literally overnight.

Note for GPS Users

A substantial number of campsites in this guide have coordinates (latitude and longitude) which can be utilized by those with GPS receivers as an additional means of navigating to the campsite. The coordinates were acquired during field research using GDA 94 map datum and are in HDDD MM.MMM format.

REMEMBER

After you have chosen your campsite we strongly recommend that you contact the park, forest or reserve office prior to your departure to obtain advice on current and upcoming conditions. For sites where a camping/entry fee is payable we recommend that you contact the land managers to obtain the current fee schedule before arrival. Be aware that some sites may require advance bookings, especially during the popular holiday periods over Christmas/ New Year and Easter. Booking requirements are detailed for these sites in the guide.

Camping in Tasmania

Tasmania is one of Australia's best state-based destinations for going camping. Now becoming increasingly popular with both interstate and overseas visitors alike, Tasmania is no longer one of Australia's best kept secrets. The word's out and people are now holidaying in the 'Island State' in unprecedented numbers, many travelling around in caravans, campervans and motorhomes. With a host of superb campsites ranging from idyllic coastal locations to secluded lakeside sites up in the Central Highlands, campers are sure to find the ideal site to pitch their tent or setup a van.

Camping is fun and a great way to experience Tasmania. Here you'll find something to suit everyone, whether you're a once a year camper, a long term traveller, an avid adventurer, a bushwalker or out four-wheel drive touring. This fully updated edition of Camping Guide to Tasmania is your comprehensive guide to camping within Tasmania's national parks, conservation areas, forest reserves and lakeside reserves. It contains details on the state's designated campsites where you can enjoy a night under the stars. From the rugged south-west wilderness to the picturesque east coast to the unique central highland lakes, there are parks and reserves that cater for all styles of camping amongst some of Australia's most beautiful and diverse landscapes. This compact state sure does offer a lot of variety for visitors to experience.

No matter what type of camping you prefer, be it a secluded walk-in campsite, car-based camping beside a river or the ocean, or with your van at a campground with amenities, you will be sure to find an ideal campsite to suit your needs amongst the 180 plus sites in this guide. You will find opportunities to relax on one of the many beautiful white sandy beaches with crystal clear water on the east coast, walk amongst the treetops and lookout over the mighty Huon River at the Tahune Forest AirWalk, take a cruise on one of the west coast's picturesque waterways, fish for trout in one of the many inland lakes and visit historic towns with rich and colourful pasts. Visitors can walk through world renown wilderness regions, marvel at the abundant wildlife including Tasmania's own devil and be captivated by towering forests. All this and much more is available in the 96 parks and reserves within this guide.

So, why not pack the tent and head off to discover the delights of Tasmania. See spectacular plants and wildlife in their natural environments (many of which are unique to Tasmania), take in the sights and sounds of the Tasmanian bush and gaze in awe at the stunning natural beauty that is to be found throughout Australia's visually spectacular island state.

Happy Camping

Craig Lewis and Cathy Savage
Kybeyan NSW

Getting to Tasmania

The majority of people travelling to Tasmania for a camping holiday either bring their own vehicle from the mainland via the Spirit of Tasmania ferry service or fly-drive, that is, fly to Tasmania and hire a campervan or motorhome. The advantage of travelling on the ferry service is that you have your own vehicle with your own camping kit.

The *Spirit of Tasmania I* and *II* travel between Melbourne and Devonport daily, leaving both Melbourne and Devonport (on days of single sailings) early evening (7.30pm) for the 10 hour overnight crossing and arrive in port early next morning (6.30am). During peak months (Oct - May) there are days with scheduled dual sailings - day and night sailings. On these days the night sailings are as detailed above and the day sailings leave at 9am (with 6.30pm arrival) or 9.30am (with 7pm arrival). You have the choice (for a cost) of a variety of sleeper cabins or 'aircraft' style sit-up seats for overnight sailings. For day sailings, you grab a seat anywhere - either inside or on deck. The ferries leave from Station Pier on Port Phillip Bay (it is well signposted) in Melbourne and from the ferry terminal at East Devonport, which is on the opposite side of the river from the main part of town.

You need to book in advance for these ferries, you can't just show up and expect to hop aboard. If travelling during the peak summer months be sure to book your passage well in advance as often the ships are fully booked for certain crossings months ahead.

There are a few issues travelling campers should be aware of when boarding the ferries. Gas bottles which are not fixed to either the vehicle or trailer must be removed and placed in the separate bottle trailer and retrieved upon disembarking. All fuel containers (jerry cans) must be emptied of fuel and filled with water, otherwise they will not be permitted on board the vessel. These will be checked at boarding. When arriving in Tasmania quarantine inspections occur and restrictions apply to carrying fresh fruit and vegetables and fresh fish products, plants and soil. These products will be confiscated.

FURTHER INFORMATION

Fares, sailing schedules, booking and further details can be had by contacting TT Lines on 1800 634 906 or online at www.spiritoftasmania.com.au
For details of what can and cannot be taken into Tasmania, Biosecurity Tasmania can be contacted on tel: 1300 368 550 or visit www.dpipwe.tas.gov.au/biosecurity-tasmania

Planning

Like many experienced campers, we've found over the years the key to hassle free camping is to follow the KIS principal – Keep It Simple. It's all about getting back to basics, enjoying the great Australian outdoors. Stick to the basics. Travel light.

Your camping holiday will be much more enjoyable with the right gear. If you are setting up a camping outfit then buy the best gear you can afford. Quality gear, such as tents and sleeping gear will serve you well over a long period if looked after.

The warmer months of the year, from around October through to April are the best times for camping along Tasmania's coastal fringe. Days are generally warm and nights mild, although Tasmania can experience the odd spell of hot weather across the state over the summer period. Remember to always pack a warm jumper and long pants, even in summer. The Highlands and Central Lakes region is popular over summer, especially with fisherfolk who flock to the numerous waterside campsites. Try the shoulder seasons here for fewer crowds. The South-West region of the state can experience extreme temperatures during winter with periods of cold wet weather and is best avoided at this time. Spring, summer and early autumn are the best times to visit here, especially if bushwalking.

Biting insects such as spiders, bees, wasps, ants, ticks or mosquitoes can turn a dream camping holiday into a nightmare. To help protect yourself from these unwelcome visitors wear long pants, long sleeve shirts and shoes and don't forget insect repellent.

Never pitch your tent directly under large trees. Those large, shady trees lining our inland rivers might look like inviting campsites but they have a habit of dropping branches without warning.

When planning your camping trip, don't head off without:

- Good maps. See 'Maps, guidebooks and passes' in this section. If you plan on venturing off the beaten track, be it bushwalking, vehicle touring or fishing, be sure to carry a detailed map of the area you plan to visit.
- A gas/liquid fuel stove. If the campsite you want to visit doesn't allow you to light a fire (be aware of summer fire restrictions across the state) or provide cooking facilities, then you will need to take your own. A small single burner gas stove is fine for 2-3 people; 2 burner stoves are a better option for families.
- Insect repellent and a first aid kit. Mosquitoes, sand flies and bugs can be a nuisance while a good first aid kit is a necessity.
- Wet weather protection. Besides personal wet weather gear, a poly tarp can be rigged up to provide protection from rain and wind.
- Plenty of fresh drinking water. Carry water with you on walks, even short ones
- If you are camping in remote areas well away from shops be sure to take enough food with you – and always pack for an extra day or two in case inclement weather etc holds you up. When you're out in the fresh air, you often have a bigger appetite, especially if you combine some swimming, bike riding or bushwalking. Kids especially get very hungry on camping trips, so make sure you include healthy nibbles.

For a detailed equipment checklist see the Equipment Checklist section.

WE COULDN'T LIVE WITHOUT...

We always travel with a 12 volt portable fridge, and have done so for the last 15 years. We have used a number of different brands over the years and have found them all to be efficient and reliable. Our current fridge is a Waeco 50 litre unit. We have our meat vacuum sealed, so run the fridge as a refrigerator, not as a freezer. Visit www.waeco.com.au

One of the best portable barbecues we have come across is the *Biji Barbi*. It consists of a round steel plate with a slight dish to allow the fat and oil to run to the centre and drip through a small hole, adding fuel to your cooking fire. There are three folding legs as well as a folding handle. The Biji Barbi is a permanent piece of our bush cooking gear. Check out www.biji-barbi.com.au

Under Cover

There is a bewildering choice of camping accommodation available today, be it a tent, camper trailer, caravan, swag or roof top tent. Your choice of camping accommodation really depends on things such as the time you'll spend using it, your budget, available vehicle space (whether it is to be stowed in the vehicle, on a roof rack or towed), the number of people to accommodate and the environment it will be used in. With the increasing use of four-wheel drives as towing vehicles, camper trailers are gaining in popularity at an amazing pace, especially the more rugged off-road units. These are often favoured by long term travellers and families who camp out regularly. Advantages of camper trailers include extra storage space, comfortable sleeping area and often extra shade and weather cover from awnings. Remember though that some destinations are out of bounds or just not practical if you are towing a trailer. Becoming increasingly more common are the number of national park campsites throughout the state which are not trailer friendly. These sites are ringed by bollards, providing a small vehicle parking space. You carry your camping gear over these to the grassed campsite.

Sleep Easy

Self-inflating camp mattresses are by far the best choice for tent-based campers and offer a comfortable nights sleep. Mattresses range from ultra light ¾ length models for bushwalkers through to heavier and more bulky double models which are perfect for vehicle based campers. We use a double self-inflating mattress in our tent, and it also doubles as our swag mattress. Self-inflating mattresses roll up to form a compact cylinder which can easily be stowed in your vehicle, or on a roof rack. Although they rarely leak, don't forget a puncture repair kit just in case. Comfortable bedding is also a must. Winter nights in Tasmania can fall below freezing, the weather is very changeable across the state's far west coast while summer on the south-east coast is far more temperate. A good, zero degrees rated sleeping bag will cover most camping scenarios. We use sleeping bags when bushwalking but prefer sheets and a doona when vehicle-based camping. And don't forget your pillow.

Now I See the Light

The quality and choice of camp lighting has improved a lot in recent years. While gas (LPG or butane) lanterns are still popular, we have found the portable 12 volt fluorescent lights to be the best all-round camp lighting. These units throw out good light with minimal current draw from your vehicle's battery. Rechargeable lanterns are another option (they can be recharged via your vehicles cigarette lighter socket) while a rechargeable torch or two takes up little room. We also take with us a good quality headlamp which is indispensible for cooking and other late night camp chores.

Lets Cook

An increasing number of national park campgrounds have gas/electric barbecues for visitor use. If you would like a campfire and a camping area has a wood fireplace then please use it – and keep your cooking fire small. A folding grate for the fire and a BBQ plate (some camping areas provide these), frying pan, a few pots with lids and a couple of billies and maybe a camp oven is all that's required for camp cooking. A pair of sturdy leather gloves and shovel are also handy. And don't forget a gas stove.

MAPS, PASSES AND PERMITS

All campsites in this guide are referenced to the Touring Map section in the back of the book (abbreviated to MR in campsite descriptions). This road atlas, which covers Tasmania in detail, is used to locate campsites along with the regional maps and national park/forest maps in this guide.

For those who require greater detail the Tasmanian Government publishes a series of four 1:250 000 scale topographic maps that cover the whole state. These are titled North-West, North-East, South-East and South-West.

There are a range of handy guides available to regional areas of Tasmania, some detailing the states top outdoor locations. Two invaluable guides for campers include National Parks, Forests & Waterways Tasmania, A Visitors Guide and Tasmania's Great Short Walks - 60 Walks Around Tasmania. These and other guides are available free from visitor information centres aboard the Spirit of Tasmania ferries as well as centres throughout Tasmania.

National Park Annual Passes

Entry fees apply to visit national parks throughout Tasmania. There are a range of park passes available to visitors, the Holiday Pass offers excellent value for visitors to the state as it covers all national parks and is valid for up to eight weeks. This pass is available for vehicle based travellers, motorcycle tourers and even those visiting on foot. Please note that the Parks Passes do not cover camping fees and/or overnight walking track fees. The Passes are available from Parks and Wildlife offices, at self-registration stations at major parks and at various other outlets including aboard the Spirit of Tasmania ferries.

For further details on the range of Park Passes available contact the individual Parks and Wildlife Service office listed in this guide, or Parks and Wildlife Tasmania head office on Tel: 1300 827 727. Alternatively, log onto the Parks and Wildlife Service Tasmania website at www.parks.tas.gov.au

Fishing

Fishing licences are required in Tasmania, contact the appropriate department for up-to-date information on licensing, rules and regulations. Sea Fisheries - Department of Primary Industry, Water and Environment Tel: 1300 720 647 or visit their website at www.dpipwe.tas.gov.au/fishing

Inland Fisheries Service Tel: 03 6165 3808 or visit the sevice's website at www.ifs.tas.gov.au

Camping Permits and Fees

Camping fees and permits are required for a number of campsites in this guide. Camping fees in national parks are generally geared to the level of facilities provided at the campsite. Depending on the campsite, fees may be payable when booking, be collected by a caretaker or be payable at a self-registration station at the site. Details on fees and permits can be found in the Further Information box for that listing, along with payment details.

For safety purposes, some remote walk-in sites or canoe access sites may require visitors to register their intentions with the land managers.

NOTE ON CAMPING FEES

The camping fees indicated in the Further Information box are correct at the time of research and generally reflect the low season fee. Peak season fees may be higher than those listed. Camping fees may rise or be introduced to areas which may have previously been free of charge. It is the responsibility of individuals to enquire with the land managers about the status of areas they wish to visit, including current fees, prior to departure.

FIRE WARNINGS AND RESTRICTIONS

On days declared total fire bans you're not allowed to have any fire in the open, this includes solid fuel fires, gas cookers or barbecues. Fire bans are generally broadcast on local radio stations and it's your responsibility to be aware of these. On days of high fire danger it may be prudent to refrain from having open fires; use gas or fuel cooking appliances instead.

To protect the natural environment and local wildlife, you may find that a number of national parks and reserves listed in this guide do not permit campfires. For these parks and reserves, it's essential that you carry your own gas/fuel stove for cooking.

Bushfires

During the bushfire season, which is generally early November to late April in Tasmania, it is vital to be fire smart. If you are out camping and a bushfire threatens seek shelter, be it in a river, stream, dam, large clearing or behind a rock outcrop and prepare a shelter from the fire's radiant heat. Keep down low to the ground and cover up. Remember, it isn't wise to try and outrun a bushfire – shelter until the main fire front has passed. Check out the Tasmania Fire Service website at www.fire.tas.gov.au for additional bushfire information.

Firewood

Wood is becoming scarce in popular camping areas. Fallen and dead timer also provides habitats for the local wildlife. If you're camping where campfires are permitted, try to purchase or collect your wood prior to arrival to the campsite. Some parks prohibit the collection of firewood within the park and some parks may have signposted firewood collection points outside the park boundary. Also, to help protect the spread of exotic weeds and pests, some national parks and reserves request that collected firewood from outside the immediate area is not to be taken into the parks.

Vegetation

Please do not cut down any vegetation, either living or dead, and do not collect or use wood that may have habitat holes. If you use a campfire you must ensure that all combustible material is clear for 4 metres, never leave the campfire unattended and always put it out with water (never with sand or dirt). Never throw cans or glass into your campfire.

Remember the average-sized campfire...

- is capable of generating over 500 Degrees of heat after burning for only three hours.
- when extinguished with sand or dirt, retains up to 100 Degrees of heat for eight hours.
- when extinguished with a bucket of water retains little or no heat after of period of ten minutes.

FURTHER INFORMATION

Tasmanian Fire Service (total fireban updates and bushfire updates)
Tel: 1800 000 699 or 03 6230 8600
Web: www.fire.tas.gov.au
All fire emergencies dial 000

GREYWATER AND SULLAGE DUMP SITES

Dumps sites may be used by caravanners, campervanners and motorhomers to conveniently dispose of greywater & chemical toilet sullage. Greywater and sullage should never be emptied into composting or pit toilets, as chemicals destroy the composting bacteria, rendering them ineffective.

- **Arthur River:** Airey Street, (Gardner Point) Edge of the World
- **Beaconsfield:** Showgrounds, Grubb Street
- **Bicheno:** Bicheno Beach opposite police station, Champ Street
- **Bridport:** Bridport Caravan Park, Bentley Street
- **Brighton:** Brighton Hotel, Midlands Highway
- **Burnie:** Cooee Point Reserve, Cooee Point Road
- **Cambridge:** Cambridge Memorial Oval, Cambridge Road
- **Campbell Town:** King Street Oval
- **Cygnet:** Burtons Reserve, off Charlton Street
- **Deloraine:** Adjacent to racecourse entry, Racecourse Drive
- **Devonport East:** Girdlestone Park Football Ground, cnr John & Caroline Streets
- **Dover:** Kent Beach Road
- **Evandale:** Morven Park, Barclay Street
- **Fingal:** located at public toilets in Talbot Street
- **Franklin:** Franklin Foreshore camping and caravan area A6 highway – see page 69
- **George Town:** Visitor Information Centre, Main Street
- **Kempton:** red toilet block at rear of Victoria Hall, Main Street
- **Kingston:** Kingston Wetlands Park, access behind Kingston Hotel at corner of Channel Hwy
- **Latrobe:** car park off Cotton Street behind supermarkets
- **Launceston:** Treasure Island Caravan Park, 94 Glen Dhu Street
- **Longford:** Riverside Caravan Park, Archer Street
- **Narawntapu National Park:** Located at Bakers Point camping area – see page 47
- **Oatlands:** Junction of Williams and Wellington Streets
- **Penguin:** corner Main and Johnsons Beach roads.
- **Pontville:** Pontville Park, Midlands Highway
- **Port Arthur:** Port Arthur Caravan Park at Garden Point, turn left off highway before town
- **Port Sorell:** Port Sorell Jetty Point
- **Rosny:** Sewage Treatment Plant off Rosny Esplande
- **Scottsdale:** North East Park Campground, A3 Highway – see page 52
- **Sheffield:** West Nook Road
- **Sorell:** Council depot, Montague Street (weekdays only)
- **St Helens:** Sportsgrounds, off Tully Street
- **St Helens:** St Helens Caravan Park, Penelope Street
- **Stanley:** Stanley Caravan Park, Wharf Road
- **Stanley:** Tatlows Beach off Wharf Road
- **Swansea:** Opposite post office at boat ramp car park, Jetty Road
- **Triabunna:** Visitor Information Centre, Cnr Charles Street and The Esplanade
- **Ulverstone:** Apex Caravan Park, Queen Street
- **Ulverstone:** end of Victoria Street near beach.
- **Waratah:** opposite Waratah Council works depot, Annie Street
- **Westbury:** Andy's Motorhome and Camper Park, Meander Valley Road – see page 35
- **Wynyard:** Wynyard Solid Waste Transfer Station, Goldie Street – 9am to 5pm seven days

TREADING SOFTLY ON TASMANIA

Tasmania's parks and reserves are some of the state's most precious and at the same time sensitive recreational resources.

When enjoying these areas, whether it be camping, walking, canoeing, cycling, car touring, 4WDing or just going bush, it's important to tread lightly on the environment.

Minimal impact camping is the way to go. When setting up camp there are a few simple guidelines, which if followed ensure that Tasmania's parks and reserves are preserved for everyone to enjoy in the future.

Minimal impact camping guidelines:

Be prepared: Plan your trip carefully and make sure your gear is in good order (for good gear tips, see 'Planning' in this section).

Camp fire safety: Use fireplaces where provided and observe any fire bans. Clear combustible material 4 metres away from the fire. Be sure the fire is out before leaving (for more, see the section 'Fire Warnings and Restrictions').

Protect plants and animals: Protect plants and animals: If possible, make your camp to avoid trampling plants or disturbing animals. Do not feed wildlife as 'human food' can cause illness and disease to animals.

Waterway care: Don't pollute waterways. Don't use soap or detergents in or close to waterways. Wash at least 100 metres from waterways.

Toilet time: Use toilets if provided. If not, bury wastes at least 100 metres away from campsites and watercourses, in a hole at least 15cm deep.

Use rubbish bins if provided or take your rubbish with you when you leave. Don't bury rubbish. Leave campsites better than you found them.

Neighbours: Be considerate of others when camping nearby.

WHAT TO PACK

Camping Equipment

- Bucket
- Chairs
- Dust pan & brush
- First Aid Kit
- Fluro light
- Ground sheet
- Head torch
- Mattress/s
- Mattress pump
- Pillows and cases
- Screen/mesh tent
- Sleeping bag
- Spare rope
- Swag
- Table
- Tent
- Tent pegs
- Tent poles
- Tent rope
- Torch
- Torch batteries
- Water container

Cooking Equipment

- Matches and/or lighter
- Firelighters
- Two burner gas stove and gas bottle
- BBQ plate
- Grill or grate
- 2 saucepans with lids
- Frying pan
- Camp oven
- Trivet - to fit camp oven
- Billy
- Tripod hanger and hooks
- Pie dish - to fit camp oven
- Pizza tray - to fit camp oven
- Camp oven lifters
- Shovel - long handled
- Leather gloves

Miscellaneous Cooking Items

- Roll of aluminium foil
- Roll of cling wrap
- Paper towel
- Plastic bottle for milk
- Plastic bottle for cordial
- Plastic bottle for extra water
- Storage containers with lids
- Zip lock bags

Personal Eating Equipment - 1 per person

- Bowl
- Fork
- Knife
- Mug
- Plate
- Spoon
- Steak Knife
- Tea spoon

Cooking Utensils

- Mixing bowls
- Measuring jug
- Tongs - short or long
- Bar-B-Q Mate
- Basting brush

- Serving spoon
- Slotted serving spoon
- Peelers
- Egg flip
- Flat grater
- Can opener with bottle opener
- Swiss Army Knife
- Flat Strainer
- Egg rings
- Large sharp knife
- Bread/Serrated edge knife
- Wooden spoons
- Cutting board
- Mesh toaster
- Measuring spoon and/or tablespoon
- Extra plate and bowl for serving
- General purpose scissors

Washing/Cleaning Equipment

- Cloth
- Clothesline and pegs
- Detergent
- Dish brush
- Garbage bags
- Scourer
- Scrubbing brush
- Sponge
- Tea towel/s
- Wash up bucket
- Washing powder for clothes

Personal Items

- Comb and/or brush
- Toothbrush
- Toothpaste
- Towel
- Face Washer
- Soap and container
- Shampoo and Conditioner
- Deodorant
- Sunblock
- Toilet paper
- Insect repellent

USEFUL RESOURCES AND CONTACTS

Parks & Wildlife Service
Tel: 1300 827 727
Web: www.parks.tas.gov.au

Parks & Wildlife Service Visitor Centres - Open 7 days
Cradle Mountain Tel: 03 6492 1110
Freycinet Tel: 03 6256 7000
Hastings Caves Tel: 03 6298 3209
Lake St Clair Tel: 03 6289 1172
Mt Field Tel: 03 6288 1149
Narawntapu Tel: 03 6428 6277

Sustainable Timber Tasmania
Tel: 03 6233 8203
Web: www.sttas.com.au

Hydro Tasmania
Tel: 1300 360 441
Web: www.hydro.com.au

Inland Fisheries Service
Tel: 03 6165 3808
Web: www.ifs.tas.gov.au

Department of Primary Industries, Parks, Water & Environment - Sea Fishing & Aquaculture
Recreational Fisheries Enquiries
Tel: 03 6165 3233 or 1300 720 647
Web: www.dpipwe.tas.gov.au/fishing

Tasmanian Fire Service
Tel: 1800 000 699 or 03 6230 8600
Web: www.fire.tas.gov.au

RACT
Roadside Assistance **Tel:** 131 111
General Enquiries **Tel:** 132 722
Web: www.ract.com.au

Transport Tasmania
General Enquiries **Tel:** 1300 135 513
Web: www.transport.tas.gov.au

Tourism Tasmania
Web: www.discovertasmania.com.au

Regional Visitor Information Centres

Bicheno
Tel: 03 6375 1500
Web: www.gsbc.tas.gov.au

Burnie
Tel: 03 6430 5831
Web: www.discoverburnie.net

Cygnet
Tel: 03 6131 4803

Deloraine
Tel: 03 6362 5280
Web: www.greatwesterntiers.net.au

Devonport
Tel: 03 6424 4466
Web: www.devonport.tas.gov.au

Evandale
Tel: 03 6391 8128

Exeter
Tel: 1800 637 989
Web: www.wtc.tas.gov.au

George Town
Tel: 03 6382 1700
Web: www.georgetown.tas.gov.au

Hobart
Tel: 03 6238 4222
Web: www.hobarttravelcentre.com.au

Huonville
Tel: 03 6264 1838
Web: www.huonvalleyvisitorcentre.com.au

Kettering
Tel: 03 6267 4494

Launceston
Tel: 1800651 827
Web: www.destinationlaunceston.com.au

Port Arthur
Tel: 03 6251 2371
Web: www.portarthur.org.au

Ross
Tel: 03 6381 5466

Scottsdale
Tel: 03 6352 4388

Sheffield
Tel: 03 6491 1179
Web: www.sheffieldcradleinfo.com.au

Stanley
Tel: 03 6458 1330

St Helens
Tel: 03 6376 1744
Web: www.bodc.tas.gov.au

Strahan
Tel: 1800 352 200
Web: www.westernwilderness.com.au

Swansea
Tel: 03 6256 5072
Web: www.gsbc.tas.gov.au

Triabunna
Tel: 03 6257 4772
Web: www.gsbc.tas.gov.au

Ulverstone
Tel: 03 6425 2839
Web: www.coasttocanyon.com.au

Wynyard
Tel: 03 6443 8330
Web: www.wondersofwynyard.com

Spirit of Tasmania (TT-Line)
Information and Reservations **Tel:** 1800 634 906
Web: www.spiritoftasmania.com.au

Bureau of Meterology
Web: www.bom.gov.au

Lake Pedder, Southwest National Park

The North-East and Flinders Island

ONE OF TASMANIA'S MOST VISITED regions, the North-East is blessed with kilometre after kilometre of stunning coastline which features pristine white sandy beaches interspersed with rugged headlands and rocky outcrops. Popular locations include the Bay of Fires Conservation Area north of St Helens and Mt William National Park, one of the North-East's more remote and beautiful national parks. At both of these locations you will find a host of picture-perfect coastal campsites.

BEST CAMPSITES!

- **Stumpys Bay: Campsite No 2**
  Mt William National Park
- **Griffin camping area**
  Saddleback Plantation
- **Cosy Corner North camping area**
  Bay of Fires Conservation Area
- **Waterhouse Point camping area**
  Waterhouse Conservation Area
- **Bakers Point camping area**
  Narawntapu National Park

In the north of the region and fronting Bass Strait is the delightful holiday destination of Bridport, while running to the north-east is Waterhouse Conservation Area—a popular fishing and camping destination over summer. This park, which offers minimal visitor facilities, offers ten camping areas to choose from, ranging from protected lakeside sites to those on headlands with stunning ocean vistas. Further to the west near Port Sorell is Narawntapu National Park, a great spot for wildlife watching. This park is also located on the coast and has ocean access as well as a protected estuary.

Away from the coast is the winter playground of Ben Lomond National Park, which offers camping while a little to the north is the delightful Griffin camping area in Saddleback Plantation. Situated beside the South Esk River, it is popular with anglers, mountain bikers and trail bike riders.

As opposed to most of Tasmania it is possible to enjoy this region all year round with its mild climate. Here you will find the warmer months tend to be the most pleasant, especially the coastal parks and reserves where campsites are at a premium over the peak summer period, as both locals and visitors flock to the region.

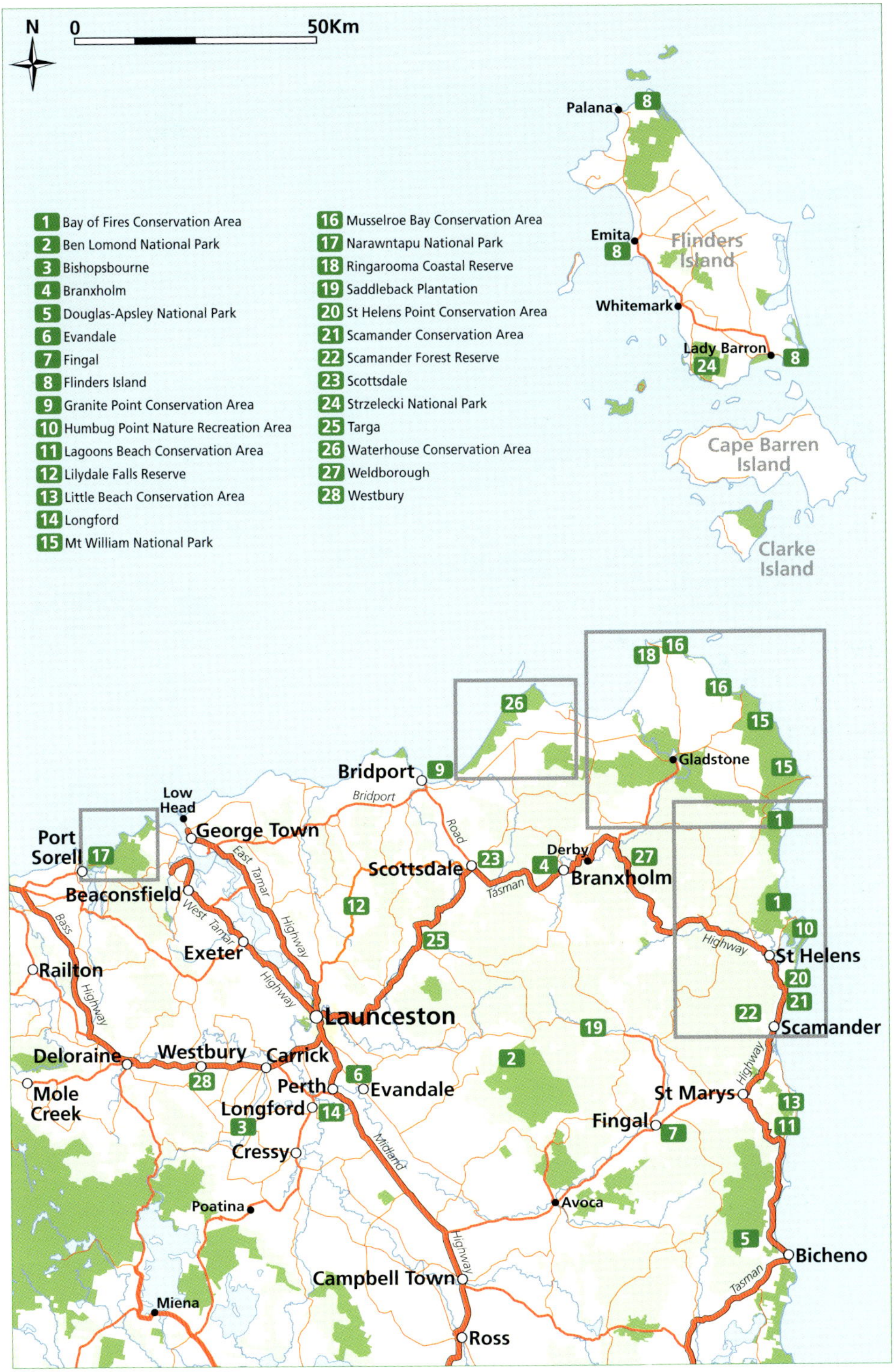
N
0
50Km
1 Bay of Fires Conservation Area
2 Ben Lomond National Park
3 Bishopsbourne
4 Branxholm
5 Douglas-Apsley National Park
6 Evandale
7 Fingal
8 Flinders Island
9 Granite Point Conservation Area
10 Humbug Point Nature Recreation Area
11 Lagoons Beach Conservation Area
12 Lilydale Falls Reserve
13 Little Beach Conservation Area
14 Longford
15 Mt William National Park
16 Musselroe Bay Conservation Area
17 Narawntapu National Park
18 Ringarooma Coastal Reserve
19 Saddleback Plantation
20 St Helens Point Conservation Area
21 Scamander Conservation Area
22 Scamander Forest Reserve
23 Scottsdale
24 Strzelecki National Park
25 Targa
26 Waterhouse Conservation Area
27 Weldborough
28 Westbury
Palana
Emita
Flinders Island
Whitemark
Lady Barron
Cape Barren Island
Clarke Island
Gladstone
Bridport
Low Head
George Town
Port Sorell
Beaconsfield
Scottsdale
Derby
Branxholm
St Helens
Scamander
Railton
Exeter
Launceston
Deloraine
Westbury
Carrick
Perth
Evandale
Mole Creek
Longford
Cressy
St Marys
Fingal
Avoca
Poatina
Bicheno
Campbell Town
Miena
Ross
Bridport Road
East Tamar Highway
West Tamar Highway
Bass Highway
Tasman Highway
Midland Highway

1 Bay of Fires Conservation Area

The southern section of the conservation area stretches along the coast from Binalong Bay in the south for 13km north to The Gardens. Located along this pristine coastline are numerous camping areas signposted off The Gardens Road, which is signposted 8km north of St Helens along Binalong Bay Road. Further north Policemans Point is situated to the south of Ansons Bay and accessed via Ansons Bay Road. The area's magnificent coastline, spectacular views, beautiful beaches and azure waters make it a popular destination for swimmers, divers and fisherfolk.

MIDDLE SECTION CAMPING AREA

Policemans Point Campground

Policemans Point is situated 5.2km east of the C843 road. Southern access from St Helens, take the C843/Ansons Bay Road for 34.5km, then take signposted road to Policemans Point. Northern access from Ansons Bay take the C843/St Helens Road 3km west of Ansons Bay, travel for 5.1km to the signposted Policemans Point road. Campsites are protected in coastal heath on the southern side of Ansons Bay mouth. Bring drinking water, firewood and chemical toilet.

GPS S:41 03.680 E:148 17.425

MR: Map 4 J5

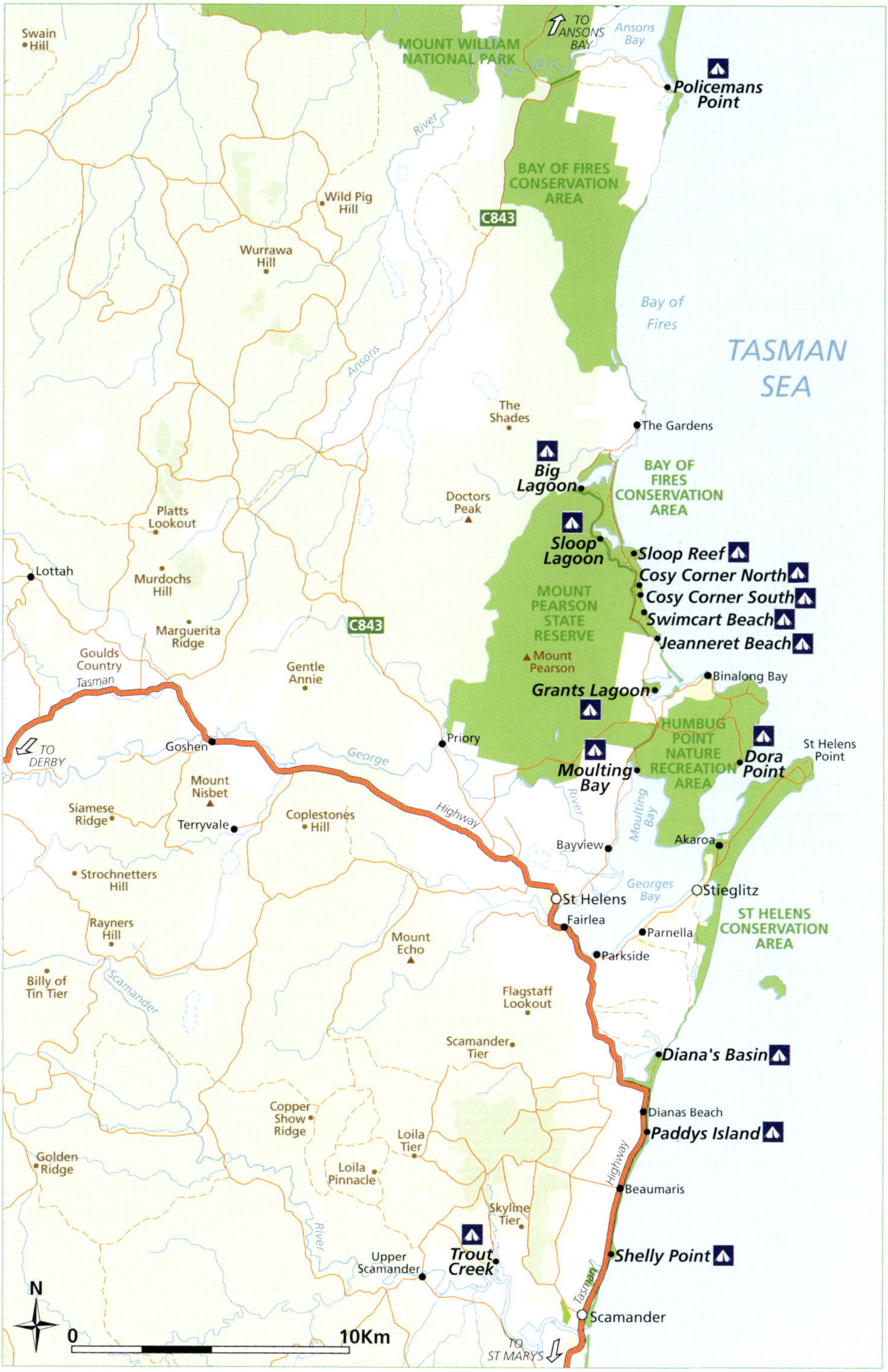

THE NORTH-EAST AND FLINDERS ISLAND

SOUTHERN SECTION CAMPING AREAS

Grants Lagoon camping area

Signposted access off The Gardens Road, 1.3km from Binalong Bay Road. Number of grassed clearings set back from water. Little shade. Suitable for big rigs. Bring drinking water and firewood.

GPS S:41 15.256 E:148 17.372

MR: Map 4 J6

Jeanneret Beach camping area

Signposted access off The Gardens Road, 3.2km from Binalong Bay Road. Bring drinking water and firewood.

GPS S:41 14.260 E:148 17.403

MR: Map 4 J6

Swimcart Beach camping area

Signposted access off The Gardens Road, 4.1km from Binalong Bay Road. Then in 400m to sites. Bring drinking water and firewood.

GPS S:41 13.743 E:148 17.047

MR: Map 4 J6

Cosy Corner South camping area

Signposted access off The Gardens Road, 5.3km from Binalong Bay Road. Then in 200m to sites. Number of sites along the coast and other sites set back in vegetation. Bring drinking water and firewood.

GPS S:41 13.419 E:148 16.966

MR: Map 4 J6

Cosy Corner South camping area

Cosy Corner North camping area

Signposted access off The Gardens Road, 5.6km from Binalong Bay Road. Then in 200m to sites. Best suited for larger vans and big rigs. Bring drinking water and firewood.

GPS S:41 13.250 E:148 16.907
MR: Map 4 J6

Sloop Reef camping area

Signposted access off The Gardens Road, 7.4km from Binalong Bay Road. Then 400m to crossroads. At crossroads road on left leads 200m to small camping area overlooking the water suitable for camper trailers and small vans. At crossroads road on right leads 200m to small camping area suitable for tent based camping. Bring drinking water, firewood and chemical toilet.

Area for camper trailers and small vans **GPS** S:41 12.547 E:148 16.728
Area for tents **GPS** S:41 12.736 E:148 16.843
MR: Map 4 J6

Sloop Lagoon camping area

Access via Old Gardens Road which is signposted off The Gardens Road, 6.3km from Binalong Bay Road. Numerous tracks off Old Gardens Road lead to bush campsites on the lagoon's shore. Bring drinking water, firewood and chemical toilet.

MR: Map 4 J6

Big Lagoon camping area

Access off The Gardens Road, 2km north of the bridge over Sloop Lagoon. Then drive in for 1km to the turn-off into Bay of Fires Conservation Area. Numerous tracks lead to bush campsites on the lagoon's shore. Bring drinking water, firewood and chemical toilet.

MR: Map 4 J6

FURTHER INFORMATION

Parks & Wildlife Service St Helens
Tel: 03 6376 1550
St Helens Visitor Centre
Tel: 03 6376 1744
Parks Pass: Not required.
Maximum stay: 4 weeks.

Cosy Corner North camping area,
Bay of Fires Conservation Area

2 Ben Lomond National Park

The Ben Lomond plateau is a popular winter destination for skiers and in summer for bushwalkers, birdwatchers and nature enthusiasts. The park is located 50km south-east of Launceston. Signposted access to the park is via the Ben Lomond Road off the C401, 13km south of Upper Blessington.

Ben Lomond camping area

Access via Ben Lomond Road, 13km south of Upper Blessington. Camping area located 1km within park boundary with six unpowered sites. Best suited for tent-based camping, small trailers and campervans. Bring firewood. Gas/fuel stove preferred.

GPS S:41 30.250 E:147 36.767

MR: Map 4 G8

Bush camping

Remote bush camping for self-sufficient bushwalkers. Contact ranger for details.

FURTHER INFORMATION

Parks & Wildlife Service Prospect

Tel: 03 6777 2179

Parks Pass: Required.

3 Bishopsbourne

The quaint village of Bishopsbourne was built on land owned by Bishop Nixon, the state's first Anglican bishop. The Anglican Church built in 1844 still stands. Bishopsbourne is located 16km west of Longford. From Longford take the C519 road, or if travelling from the north take the C513 road from Carrick.

Bishopsbourne Recreational Ground

Signposted access to the recreational ground in Bishopsbourne. Designated area for fully self-contained caravans, motorhomes and campervans ie: units must have own fresh water storage, sealed grey water holding tank, sealed black water.

MR: Map 7 C1

FURTHER INFORMATION

Northern Midlands Council

Tel: 03 6397 7303

Web: www.northernmidlands.tas.gov.au

Camping permit: Camping permit required, can be obtained online.

Maximum stay: 48 hours.

4 Branxholm

Situated on the B52 road, Branxholm is 25km east of Scottsdale and 8km west of Derby. Visit a hop farm or take a gemstone tour.

Branxholm camping ground

Situated beside the Ringarooma River, on the Tasman Highway in Branxholm Bring drinking water. Coin operated showers.

GPS S:41 10.096 E:147 44.221

MR: Map G6

FURTHER INFORMATION

Dorset Council

Tel: 03 6352 6500

Web: www.northeasttasmania.com.au

Maximum stay: 4 weeks.

5 Douglas-Apsley National Park

Situated north of Bicheno. Take the short walk to Apsley Waterhole or the 3-hour Apsley Gorge circuit. Those who prefer longer walks can walk the 3-day Leeaberra Track - this walk should be undertaken in a north to south direction. Access to the southern section is via Rosedale Road off the Tasman Highway, 4km north of Bicheno. Access to the northern section (and start of the 3-day walk) is via the gravel E Road off the Tasman Highway, 4km north of Bicheno.

Apsley Waterhole camping area

Located 11km north-west of Bicheno. Signposted access off Rosedale Road. Park at car park and walk 200m into campsite. Water available from river, boil first. Gas/fuel stove preferred.

MR: Map 8 I3

Heritage Falls & Tevelein Falls camping areas

Walk-in sites along the Leeaberra Track. Access start of walk from north of park. Self-sufficient bushwalkers. Bring drinking water. Gas/fuel stove only. Obtain large scale maps and contact ranger for further details.

FURTHER INFORMATION

Parks & Wildlife Service Freycinet

Tel: 03 6256 7000

Parks Pass: Required.

Fire Restrictions: Solid fuel fire ban between 1 October and April 30. Gas/fuel stove only during this period, unless days of total fire ban. Firewood collection in park is prohibited.

NB: To help reduce spread of Root Rot, please walk Leeaberra Track from north to south and clean boots and tent pegs before and after visiting.

6 Evandale

The historic village of Evandale is situated on the South Esk River. Home to a range of unspoiled heritage buildings, the village is a National Trust classified Georgian village. Every February Evandale holds the National Penny Farthing Championships, whilst the Evandale Markets are held every Sunday where local produce and crafts are on display. Evandale is accessed via the B41 highway and is 23km south of Launceston.

Falls Park

Located on Logan Road in Evandale. Signposted access. Designated area for fully self-contained caravans, motorhomes and campervans ie: units must have own fresh water storage, sealed grey water holding tank, sealed black water.

GPS S:41 34.267 E:147 15.233
MR: Map 3 E8

FURTHER INFORMATION

Northern Midlands Council
Tel: 03 6397 7303
Web: www.northernmidlands.tas.gov.au
Camping permit: Camping permit required, can be obtained online.

Evandale Visitor Information Centre
Tel: 03 6391 8128
Web: www.evandaletasmania.com
Maximum stay: 24 hours. Overnight stops only available Monday to Friday nights.

7 Fingal

The mining village of Fingal is located to the west of St Marys on the A4 highway. Located in the village are a number of historic buildings.

Fingal Park camping area

Signposted access along the A4 highway in Fingal. Large grassed area for tent-based campers. Childrens playground. Power available. Sullage dump site.

GPS S:41 38.367 E:147 58.000
MR: Map 8 H1

FURTHER INFORMATION

Fingal Valley Neighbourhood Community House
Tel: 03 6374 2344
Maximum stay: 2 nights.

8 Flinders Island

Flinders Island is the largest of the 70 islands that make up the Fureaux Group. The island has plenty to offer the nature lover, wildlife spotter and bushwalker. The Fureaux Group is one of the richest fishing areas in Australia. Access to the island is via air or sea. There is no public transport on the island, vehicles and bicycles can be hired.

Photo courtesy of Flinders Tourism Association/John de la Roche

Flinders Island Castle Rock

Yellow Beach Coastal Reserve camping area

Located 2km east of Lady Barron. From Lady Barron take the signposted Franklin Parade, and then take the signposted Pot Boil Road to the signposted beach access. Bring drinking water and firewood. Gas/fuel stove preferred.
MR: Map 9 D5

Allports Beach camping area

Sheltered campsite among trees opposite the beach, located 21km north of Whitemark. Signposted access to Allport Beach is off Port Davies Road, south-west of Emita. Bring drinking water and firewood. Gas/fuel stove preferred.
MR: Map 9 B4

Lillies Bay camping area

Camping area on the beach. Access to Lillies Bay is signposted off Port Davies Road south-west of Emita. Good snorkelling area. Bring drinking water and firewood. Gas/fuel stove preferred.

MR: Map 9 B4

North East River camping area

Located 15km north-east of Killiecrankie. Numerous access tracks lead off the North East Road to campsites beside the river, 200m from the river mouth. Bring drinking water and firewood. NB: Be aware of undertows when swimming. Gas/fuel stove preferred.

MR: Map 9 C2

FURTHER INFORMATION

Flinders Island Visitor Information Centre

Tel: 03 6359 2217

Web: www.visitflindersisland.com.au

Photo courtesy of Flinders Tourism Association/Gary Sykes

North East River

GETTING TO FLINDERS ISLAND

Vehicle-based campers can access Flinders Island via the freight and passenger vessels operated by Furneaux Freight based at Bridport in the north-east of Tasmania. This service operates every Monday (unless a public holiday then on the Tuesday) from Bridport and returns from Flinders Island every Tuesday. Contact Furneaux Freight on 03 6356 1753 or visit www.furneauxfreight.com.au

Access to Flinders Island is also possible via air with a number of companies. Flinders Island Aviation have a regular service between Bridport and Flinders Island, phone 03 6359 3641 or visit www.flindersislandaviation.com Sharp Airlines have regular flights from Launceston and Essendon (Melbourne) to Flinders Island for all details tel: 1300 556 694 or visit www.sharpairlines.com.au Alternatively contact Flinders Island Visitor Information Centre, tel: 03 6359 2217, for further details.

Once on Flinders Island there are vehicle and bicycle hire facilities available.

9 Granite Point Conservation Area

Granite Point Conservation Area is west of Bridport on Anderson Bay. The Bridport Caravan Park is within the conservation area and offers a beachside location. Access is signposted on Bentley Street in Bridport. Due to park layout, access for some larger vans could be tricky. Bridport is accessed off the B82 Road and is 58km east of George Town and 21km north of Scottsdale.

Bridport Caravan Park

Signposted access via Bentley Street in Bridport. Campsites situated in natural coastal vegetation. Gas BBQs for hire. Camp fires allowed, bring own fire pot and firewood. Laundry facilities.

GPS S:40 59.769 E:147 23.296

MR: Map 3 E5

FURTHER INFORMATION

Bridport Caravan Park

Tel: 03 6356 1227. Bookings recommended for Easter, Christmas and New Year.

Web: www.bridportcaravanapark.com.au

Camping fees: Powered and unpowered sites available. Contact Bridport Caravan Park for current fees.

10 Humbug Point Nature Recreation Area

Large area situated on Georges Bay, with good access to the water. Access is signposted off Binalong Bay Road north of St Helens. The surrounding coastal vegetation and bay are visited by numerous bird species. This area is popular with bushwalkers and birdwatchers.

Moulting Bay camping area

Signposted access off Binalong Bay Road, 7km north of St Helens. Then drive in 900m to the well sheltered camping area. Suitable for big rigs. Beach boat launch. Bring drinking water and firewood. Gas/fuel stove preferred.

GPS S:41 16.880 E: 148 16.850

MR: Map 4 J7

Dora Point camping area

Signposted access off Binalong Bay Road, 8.2km north of St Helens, then 4.7km into camping area. Number of sheltered sites among coastal heath. Bring drinking water and firewood. Gas/fuel stove preferred.

GPS S:41 16.707 E:148 19.515

MR: Map 4 J7

FURTHER INFORMATION

Parks & Wildlife Service St Helens

Tel: 03 6387 5510

Parks Pass: Not required.

Maximum stay: 4 weeks.

11 Lagoons Beach Conservation Area

Situated east of St Marys and north of the A4, this coastal location offers visitors fishing and swimming opportunities.

Lagoons Beach camping area

Signposted access on the A3 highway. Access tracks are 1.9km and 2.3km north of the A3 and A4 junction. Spacious area behind beach stretching for 700m. Suitable for big rigs. Bring drinking water and firewood.

GPS S:41 39.034 E:148 17.713

MR: Map 8 J1

FURTHER INFORMATION

Parks & Wildlife Service Freycinet

Tel: 03 6256 7000

Parks Pass: Not required.

NB: Collection of firewood is prohibited in this area. Bring own firewood.

12 Lilydale Falls Reserve

Access to this small, delightful reserve is signposted 2.4km north of Lilydale on the B81 highway. From the camping area there is a short walk to the falls. A children's playground is also located here.

Lilydale Falls camping area

Signposted access 2.4km north of Lilydale on the B81 highway. Vehicle-based stays are limited to car parking area. For tent-based campers, carry gear short distance to grassy sites. Some firewood supplied. Gas/fuel stove preferred.

GPS S:41 13.903 E:147 12.514

MR: Map 3 D6

FURTHER INFORMATION

Lilydale Newsagent & Take Away (Yummies)

Tel: 03 6395 1156

Maximum stay: 2 nights.

13 Little Beach Conservation Area

This coastal conservation area is situated east of St Marys and the A4 Highway. Access is signposted along the A3 highway, between the highway's southern and northern junctions with the A4 highway. Visitors can enjoy coastal views, swim and fish. This low lying area is subject to water inundation and flash flooding and may be closed at times of high water and/or wet weather.

Little Beach camping area

Signposted access on the A3 highway. Approaching from the south; access is 5.1km north of the A3 and A4 junction. Approaching from the north; access is 17.5km south of the A3 and A4 junction. Grassed sites beside the river. Walk to the beach. Bring drinking water and firewood.

GPS S:41 37.541 E:148 18.704

MR: Map 8 J1

FURTHER INFORMATION

Parks & Wildlife Service Freycinet

Tel: 03 6256 7000

Parks Pass: Not required.

NB: Collection of firewood is prohibited in this area. Bring own firewood.

14 Longford

This historic and picturesque town is located west of the Midland Highway with access signposted off the highway, 20km south of Launceston. The town was established by free settlers in 1807, many of whom were provided with free convict labour. The toil of these convicts are still on show today with numerous convict-built houses about the town and surrounds.

Longford Riverside Caravan Park

Signposted access along Archer Street in Longford. Laundry facilities. Portable fireplaces are available from the office, with some firewood supplied.

GPS S:41 35.433 E:147 07.500

MR: Map 8 D1

FURTHER INFORMATION

Longford Riverside Caravan Park

Tel: 03 6391 1470

Web: www.longfordriversidecaravanpark.com

Camping fees: Unpowered from $30.00 per site/night for 2 people. Powered from $36.00 per site/night for 2 people.

15 Mt William National Park

Located in the far north-east of the region, Mt William National Park is home to a wonderful selection of beaches with fishing, diving and swimming opportunities, along with excellent wildlife viewing, beautiful coastal scenery and plenty of great bushwalks. See Forester Kangaroos grazing at dusk and dawn along the Forester Kangaroo Scenic Drive. The Eddystone Point Lighthouse is located in the south of the park and is accessed along the C846 road, which is signposted 3.4km west of Ansons Bay off the C843 road. The northern section of the park is accessed along the C845. To access the park from Gladstone take the C843 east for 8.1km, then take the C845 north for 8km to the park's information and self-registration booth. If travelling from the south, access can be had from St Helens by following the unsealed C843 north for 39.6km to the Ansons Bay Road, then turn west onto the C843 for 18.8km to the C845 road.

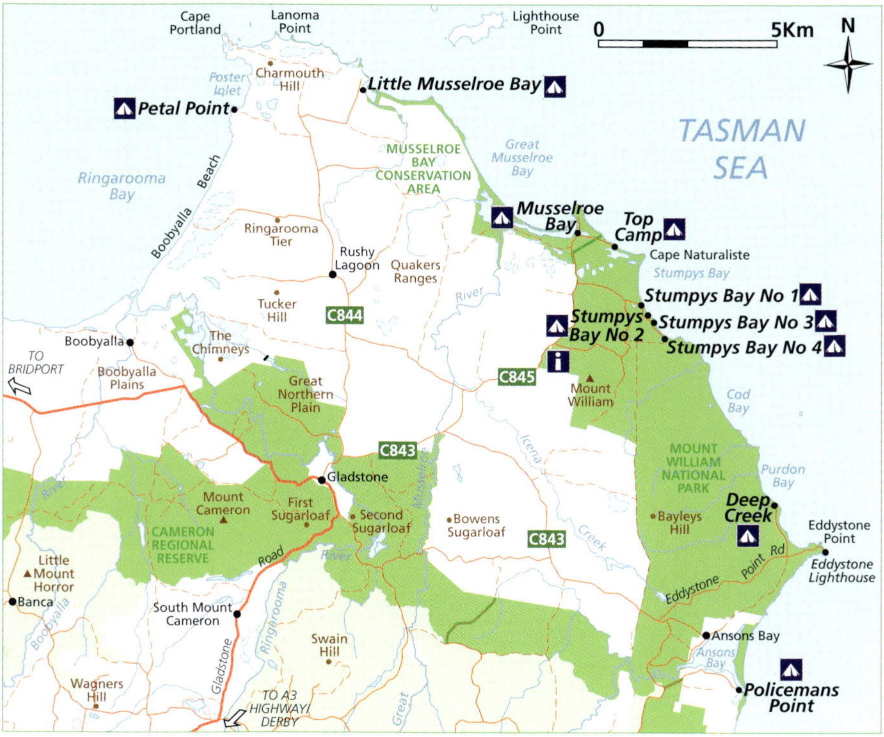

NORTHERN CAMPING AREAS

Top Camp campground

Signposted access along the C845, 7.9km north of the park information and self-registration booth. Then 2.3km east into open campsite with limited shade. Bring drinking water and firewood. Gas/fuel stove preferred.

GPS S:40 50.575 E:148 12.203

MR: Map 4 J4

Stumpys Bay: Campsite No 1

Signposted access 7.9km along the Forester Kangaroo Drive. The Forester Kangaroo Drive starts 1.1km north of the park information and self-registration booth. Access to campsite is signposted 800m east of the Forester Kangaroo Drive. Bring drinking water and firewood. Gas/fuel stove preferred.

GPS S:40 52.285 E:148 13.303
MR: Map 4 J4

Stumpys Bay: Campsite No 2

Signposted access 7.9km along the Forester Kangaroo Drive. Access track is signposted 400m past access track to Campsite No 1. This well-sheltered area is best suited for tent based camping. Bring drinking water. Gas/fuel stove only. Generators prohibited in this area.

GPS S:40 52.598 E:148 13.581
MR: Map 4 J4

Stumpys Bay: Campsite No 3

Signposted access 7.9km along the Forester Kangaroo Drive. Access track is signposted 1km past access track to Campsite No 2. Suitable for small vans. Open sites, not as well shaded or protected as Campsite Nos 1 and 2. 4WD beach boat ramp. Bore water available, suitable for washing only. Bring drinking water and firewood. Gas/fuel stove preferred.

GPS S:40 52.758 E:148 13.753
MR: Map 4 J4

Stumpys Bay: Campsite No 4

Signposted access 7.9km along the Forester Kangaroo Drive. Access track is signposted 1.4km past access track to Campsite No 3. Open area with some protected sites. Shelter and gas BBQ in adjacent day use area. Bring drinking water. Gas/fuel stove only.

GPS S:40 53.276 E:148 14.244
MR: Map 4 J4

TOTAL FIRE BANS

On days that are declared a total fire ban it is illegal to light any fire in the open, in tents and in canvas camping trailers. This includes any naked flame (portable stoves, gas and solid fuel BBQ). It's your responsibility to be aware of which fire district your campsite falls under. Fire bans are usually broadcast on the local radio station.

Stumpys Bay Campsite No4

SOUTHERN CAMPING AREA

Deep Creek camping area

Signposted access 9.5km along the C846 (Eddystone Point Road), then drive 3.3km north to the campsite. The C846 (Eddystone Point Road) is signposted off the C843 road 3.4km west of Ansons Bay. Bring drinking water and firewood. Gas/fuel stove preferred.

GPS S:40 58.194 E:148 18.726
MR: Map 4 J4

FURTHER INFORMATION

Parks & Wildlife Service St Helens
Tel: 03 6387 5510
Parks Pass: Required.
Camping fees: From $13.00 per site/night up to 2 people. Fees payable at self-registration stations.

16 Musselroe Bay Conservation Area

This popular birdwatching area is situated to the north and west of Mt William National Park. The north-western section of Musselroe Bay Conservation Area is accessed along the C844 (Cape Portland Road), whilst the eastern section, which is north of Mt William National Park, can be accessed from Gladstone by following the C843 and the C845 roads.

Little Musselroe Bay camping area

Located in the north-western part of the conservation area. Access is signposted 27.4km along the C844 (Cape Portland) road north of Gladstone. Then in 200m to the camping area with some sheltered sites on edge of the bay. Suitable for off-road camper trailers and caravans. Vehicle access only possible from Christmas to Easter. At other times site is walk-in only from the C844 road. Bring drinking water and firewood.

GPS S:40 45.982 E:148 02.018
MR: Map 4 I3

Musselroe Bay camping area

Located in the eastern section of the conservation area, 24km north-east of Gladstone and 100m north of the Mt William National Park Top Camp access road. Access is signposted along the C845 road, 7.9km north of Mt William National Park information and self-registration booth. Number of both open and sheltered campsites. Suitable for big rigs. Boat ramp nearby. Bring drinking water and firewood. Please use current fire sites, do not make new sites.

GPS S:40 50.155 E:148 10.659
MR: Map 4 J4

FURTHER INFORMATION

Parks & Wildlife Service St Helens
Tel: 03 6387 5510
Parks Pass: Not required.
Maximum stay: 4 weeks at Musselroe Bay camping area.

17 Narawntapu National Park

Located 40km east of Devonport, access to the park is signposted along the C740 road which is signposted off the B71 highway south-east of Devonport. Narawntapu National Park has a varied landscape of coastal inlets and beaches, sand dunes, wetlands and lagoons and the low ranges of Asbestos Range. These environments support a varied plant and animal life, with Forester kangaroos, Bennetts wallabies and common wombats seen grazing on the park's grasslands at dusk. Visitors to the park can enjoy bushwalking, safe beaches for swimming, water-skiing, and fishing as well as nature study and birdwatching, bike riding and horse riding. Please note that all bike riders are to stay to vehicle roads only, and conditions apply for horse riding. Check with park office for details.

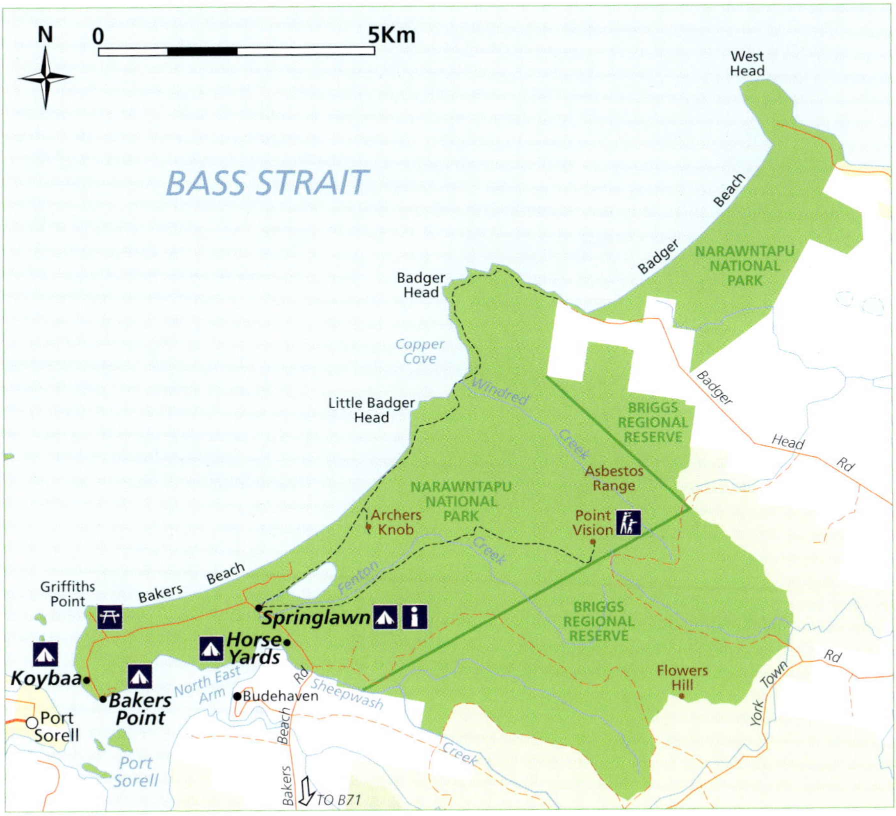

Day Use Area Only
No Camping

Bakers Point camping area, Narawntapu National Park

Horse Yards camping area

Signposted along park road, 600m in from park entrance. Limited drinking water. Some firewood supplied. Campers with horses must camp with horse and give notice 48 hours prior to arrival, conditions apply.

GPS S:41 09.224 E:146 36.588

MR: Map 3 A6

Koybaa camping area

Signposted access along main park road, 4km west of the Ranger Station. Tent based camping with 12 sites, carry gear over bollards. Walk to beach. Gas/fuel stove only. Bring drinking water.

GPS S:41 09.591 E:146 33.879

MR: Map 3 A6

Springlawn camping area

Signposted access along park road, 1km from park entrance and 100m past Ranger Station. Grassed area with 14 powered sites. Suitable for big rigs. Drinking water supplied, boil first. Token-operated hot showers, token from park office.

GPS S:41 08.907 E:146 36.127

MR: Map 3 A6

Springlawn camping area

Bakers Point camping area

Signposted access along park road, 4.5km west of Ranger Station. Large, scenic camping area along the foreshore with 36 sites, of which 16 are suitable for camper trailers, caravans and motorhomes. Most sites suitable for campervans. Boat ramp nearby. Portaloo waste collection station located here. Drinking water, boil first. Firewood supplied. Gas/fuel stove preferred.

GPS S:41 09.762 E:146 34.095

MR: Map 3 A6

FURTHER INFORMATION

Parks & Wildlife Service Narawntapu

Tel: 03 6428 6277

Parks Pass: Required.

Camping fees: From $13.00 per site/night up to 2 people. Powered sites at Springlawn CA from $16.00 per site/night for up to 2 people. Fees payable at self-registration station at Ranger Station.

18 Ringarooma Coastal Reserve

Situated on the north-east tip of the island on Ringarooma Bay. Access to the reserve is signposted off the Cape Portland Road from Gladstone. The campsite is situated at the northern end of Boobyalla Beach.

Petal Point camping area

Signposted access 21km along the C844 (Cape Portland Road) north of Gladstone, then 4.5km west into start of camping areas. Numerous tracks lead to campsites among vegetation and to open, exposed sites with great ocean views. Suitable for off-road camper trailers and caravans, as access road can be rough. Bring drinking water and firewood. Please use current fire sites, do not make new sites or carry own fire bin. Gas/fuel stove preferred.

GPS S:40 46.638 E:147 56.888

MR: Map 4 H3

FURTHER INFORMATION

Parks & Wildlife Service Scottsdale Field Centre

Tel: 03 6778 5820

Parks Pass: Not required.

19 Saddleback Plantation

Saddleback Plantation is located to the west of Mathinna and home to the popular Griffin camping area. This large grassy area is situated beside the South Esk River, well known for trout fishing. Griffin camping area is located on the gravel Griffin Park Road which can be accessed off the C401 Road (west end) or the C423 road (east end).

Griffin camping area

Numerous access tracks signposted along Griffin Road, 2km, 3.5km and 5.2km west of the C423 road. Griffin Road is signposted off the C423 road 1.7km north of Mathinna. This camping area is a favourite site for trail bike riders, especially from December to Easter. Forest harvesting does occur in these regions, and the camping area may be closed at these times. Bring drinking water and firewood.

GPS S:41 27.966 E:147 51.087

MR: Map 4 G8

South Esk River picnic and camping area

Located at junction of C423 and Griffin Road, 1.7km north of Mathinna and the B43. Lovely grassed sites beside the South Esk River. Bring drinking water and firewood.

GPS S:41 27.826 E:147 53.428

MR: Map 4 H8

FURTHER INFORMATION

Forestry Tasmania Scottsdale

Tel: 03 6352 6466

Halls Falls near Pyengana

20 St Helens Point Conservation Area

Situated to the south of St Helens the conservation area offers fishing, swimming, surfing and canoeing. Numerous campsites located on the eastern foreshore between basin and beach. Please note camping is only permitted at the designated camping area at Dianas Basin, not at St Helens Point.

Dianas Basin camping area

Signposted access off the A3 highway, 3.9km north of Beaumaris and 9km south of St Helens. Then drive in 500m to an access track on left which leads to open campsites, or drive a further 900m to area with numerous campsites protected in among the trees with shade. Bring drinking water and firewood.

Open area **GPS** S:41 22.543 E:148 17.267
Shaded area **GPS** S:41 22.223 E:148 17.574
MR: Map 4 J7

FURTHER INFORMATION

Parks & Wildlife Service St Helens
Tel: 03 6387 5510
Parks Pass: Not required.
Maximum stay: 4 weeks.

21 Scamander Conservation Area

Scamander Conservation Area stretches along the east coast from Falmouth in the south, north to Dianas Basin, protecting the coastal foreshore. The discovery of middens and tools provides evidence of a rich Aboriginal history.

Paddys Island camping area

Signposted access off the A3 highway, 2.5km north of Beaumaris. Small site behind vegetation beside road. Bring drinking water and firewood.

GPS S:41 23.718 E:148 17.346

MR: Map 4 J7

Shelly Point camping area

Signposted access off the A3 highway, 2.1km south of Beaumaris. Then 400m into sheltered camping area among vegetation close to road. Suitable for smaller caravans and campervans.

NB: Parking area near beach is day use only. Bring drinking water and firewood.

GPS S:41 26.068 E:148 16.427

MR: Map 4 J8

FURTHER INFORMATION

Parks & Wildlife Service St Helens

Tel: 03 6387 5510

Parks Pass: Not required.

Maximum stay: 4 weeks.

22 Scamander Forest Reserve

This forest reserve is situated north-west of Scamander and south-west of Beaumaris on the banks of Scamander River. Fish for bream or enjoy the quiet surrounds. Access from Beaumaris is via Skyline Drive which is signposted off the A3 highway at the tavern. Alternative access from Scamander is via the signposted C421 road. Have a good insect repellant packed in your gear.

Trout Creek camping area

Signposted access on Trout Creek Road. From Beaumaris take Skyline Drive for 700m, turn left into road signposted to Trout Creek. Follow this for 400m to next junction signposted to Trout Creek. Turn left, campsite is 3.3km along this road. From Scamander take the C421 road, which is signposted just south of Scamander, and follow it for 7km. Turn right into signposted road to Trout Creek, follow this for 5.2km to junction signposted to Trout Creek. Turn right, campsite is 3.3km along this road. Shaded, grassed camping area beside the river. Bring drinking water and firewood.

GPS S:41 26.244 E:148 13.595

MR: Map 4 J8

FURTHER INFORMATION

Forestry Tasmania Scottsdale

Tel: 03 6352 6466

Trout Creek camping area, Scamander Forest Reserve

23 Scottsdale

Scottsdale is located on the A3 highway, 63km north-east of Launceston. Regarded as the hub of the north-east, it is surrounded by some of the state's richest forest and agricultural country. Visit the Forest EcoCentre. Beside the campground is a pleasant park and pond where ducks feed and maybe even a platypus could be spotted.

Northeast Park Campground

Signposted access on the A3 highway, 1km south-east of Scottsdale. Coin operated showers. Gas/fuel stove only.

GPS S:41 09.917 E:147 31.367

MR: Map 3 F6

FURTHER INFORMATION

Scottsdale Visitor Information Centre

Tel: 03 6352 6520

Web: www.northeasttasmania.com.au

Maximum stay: 14 days.

24 Strzelecki National Park

Situated in the south-west corner of Flinders Island, Strzelecki National Park covers an area over 4200 hectares. The park has magnificent views of the surrounding islands and the coastline, and is home to tall granite peaks, beautiful wildflowers and local wildlife. Visitors can enjoy excellent swimming, fishing, diving and snorkelling. Access to the park is signposted along the B85 (Lady Barron Road) south of Whitemark. **See page 33 for access information to Flinders Island.**

Photo courtesy of Flinders Tourism Association/John de la Roche

Trousers Point camping area

Signposted access along the C806 road, 15km south of the Lady Barron Road. The C806 road is signposted off the Lady Barron Road south of Whitemark and north-west of Lady Barron. Some firewood supplied. Gas/fuel stove preferred.

MR: Map 9 C5

FURTHER INFORMATION

Parks & Wildlife Service Strzelecki National Park

Tel: 03 6359 2217

Parks Pass: Required.

25 Targa

Targa is on the A3 highway, 30km north-east of Launceston and 30km southwest of Scottsdale.

Myrtle Park Recreation Ground

Access signposted along the A3 highway, 30km south of Scottsdale. Lovely, large area with grassed, shady, sites beside the river. Some sites are open and unshaded. Suitable for big rigs. Bring drinking water. Some firewood supplied. Kiosk, playground, tennis court.

GPS S:41 18.633 E:147 21.850

MR: Map 3 E7

FURTHER INFORMATION

Launceston City Council

Tel: 03 6323 3000. Bookings recommended from November to end April.

Camping fees: From $10.00 per couple/ family/night.

NB: Onsite caretaker, contact council for current contact number to make bookings.

26 Waterhouse Conservation Area

This large conservation area stretches from the coast inland to protect a range of vegetation including heathland and the permanent deep water lagoons of Blackmans Lagoon, Big Waterhouse and Little Waterhouse lakes. Waterhouse Conservation Area is home to diverse bird and wildlife, including a number of threatened birds and mammals, as well as the dwarf galaxias, a rare freshwater fish. There are two access roads into Waterhouse Conservation Area. Access to the south-western section and Blackmans Lagoon is signposted off the B82 (Waterhouse Road) 23km east of Bridport and 38km west of Gladstone. The other road, which accesses the majority of the recreation areas is Homestead Road, which is signposted off the B82, 26.3km east of Bridport and 35km west of Gladstone. All roads within Waterhouse Conservation Area are unsealed and not regularly maintained, these roads can be rough at times. It is recommended that conventional vehicles, campervans, caravans and motorhomes contact the Parks and Wildlife Field Centre to check conditions. Visitors to Waterhouse Conservation Area can utilize the 4WD beach boat launches, go fishing, boating and sailing, as well as bird and wildlife spotting.

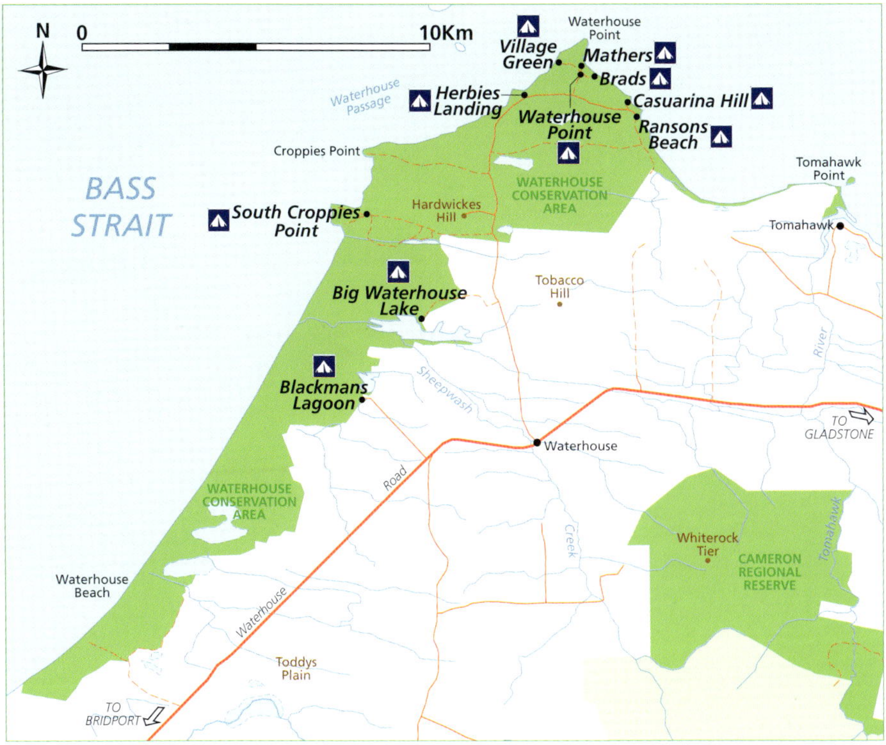

Blackmans Lagoon camping area

Signposted access along the B82 (Waterhouse Road), 23km east of Bridport and 3.3km west of Homestead Road. Then drive in 2.6km to camping area at southern end of the lagoon among pine trees. Camp only in signposted area. Best suited for camper trailers, caravans, motorhomes and campervans. Boat ramp nearby. 4WD beach access for surf fishing from campsite. Bring drinking water and firewood. Gas/fuel stove preferred.

GPS S:40 54.769 E:147 35.714

MR: Map 3 F4

Big Waterhouse Lake camping area

Signposted access 4.3km along Homestead Road, then drive in a westerly direction for 2.6km to the camping area with a few cleared sites among the vegetation on the northern shore of the lake. Homestead Road is signposted off the B82 (Waterhouse Road), 26.3km east of Bridport and 35km west of Gladstone. Bring drinking water and firewood. Gas/fuel stove preferred.

GPS S:40 53.524 E:147 36.948

MR: Map 4 G4

Shack near Big Waterhouse Lake

South Croppies Point camping area

Signposted access along Homestead Road, 2km north of Big Waterhouse Lake access track. Then drive in a westerly direction for 1.7km to Y-junction. There are a number of cleared bush campsites along the track to the left and track to the right at this junction. Recommended to bring own portable toilet. Bring drinking water and firewood. Gas/fuel stove preferred.

GPS S:40 51.959 E:147 35.726
MR: Map 4 G4

Herbies Landing camping area

Signposted access along Homestead Road, 4.6km north of South Croppies Point access track. Small area close to the road suitable for three sites. Beach boat launch. Recommended to bring own portable toilet. Bring drinking water and firewood. Gas/fuel stove preferred.

GPS S:40 50.111 E:147 39.005
MR: Map 4 G4

Waterhouse Point camping area

Signposted access along Homestead Road, 1.4km east of Herbies Landing access track. Then drive north for 700m to track junction. Dispersed bush camping is available in this vicinity and along the access track to the east. Bring drinking water and firewood. Gas/fuel stove preferred.

GPS S:40 49.826 E:147 40.412
MR: Map 4 G3

Brads camping area

Accessed via the signposted access track to Waterhouse Point, which is 1.4km east of Herbies Landing. At the junction 700m north of Homestead Road, turn right and drive in an easterly direction for 400m to the camping area. Beach boat launch. Bring drinking water and firewood. Gas/fuel stove preferred.

GPS S:40 49.826 E:147 40.412
MR: Map 4 G3

Village Green camping area

Accessed via the signposted access track to Waterhouse Point, which is 1.4km east of Herbies Landing. At the junction 700m north of Homestead Road, turn left and drive in a westerly direction for 800m to the open, grassed camping area with limited shade. Beach boat launch. Bring drinking water and firewood. Gas/fuel stove preferred.

GPS S:40 49.613 E:147 39.685
MR: Map 4 G3

Mathers camping area

Accessed via the signposted access track to Waterhouse Point, which is 1.4km east of Herbies Landing. At the junction 700m north of Homestead Road, continue straight ahead in a northerly direction for 100m to the small camping area among coastal vegetation with some shaded and protected sites. Beach boat launch. Bring drinking water and firewood. Gas/fuel stove preferred.

GPS S:40 49.662 E:147 40.141
MR: Map 4 G3

Ransons Beach

Casuarina Hill camping area

Signposted access along Homestead Road, 1.7km east of Waterhouse Point access track. Then drive in a northerly direction for 400m to the small protected camping area. Access track is steep and rutted. Bring drinking water and firewood. Gas/fuel stove preferred.

GPS S:40 50.208 E:147 41.107
MR: Map 4 G3

Ransons Beach camping area

Accessed along Homestead Road 200m east of the Casuarina Hill access track. Small area suitable for one or two tent sites, close to private shacks. Beach boat launch. 4WD beach access seasonally closed from December 1 to weekend after Easter. Recommended to bring own portable toilet. Bring drinking water and firewood. Gas/fuel stove preferred.

GPS S:40 50.424 E:147 41.282
MR: Map 4 G3

FURTHER INFORMATION

Parks & Wildlife Service Scottsdale Field Centre
Tel: 03 6352 6421
Parks Pass: Not required.
Maximum stay: 4 weeks.
NB: Beach driving is possible in the designated areas and/or the launching and retrieval of boats, contact Parks and Wildlife Service Scottsdale Field Centre for details.

27 Weldborough

Located on the A3 highway, 42km north-west of St Helens. Weldborough has a colourful past. Popular gem fossicking area nearby.

Weldborough Hotel camping ground

Located on the Tasman Highway in Weldborough, 21km south-east of Derby and 42km north-west of St Helens. Shady grassed area behind the historic Weldborough Hotel. Bring drinking water, firewood and own fire pot/bin.

GPS S:41 11.659 E:147 54.285

MR: Map 4 H6

FURTHER INFORMATION

Weldborough Hotel

Tel: 03 6354 2223

Web: www.weldborough.com.au

Camping fees: From $10.00 per person/night. Power available, surcharge applicable.

28 Westbury

Westbury is located along the Meander Valley Road (Old Bass Highway) 16km east of Deloraine and 35km west of Launceston. Andy's Bakery Cafe offers camping behind the bakery. The bakery is open 24 hours.

Andy's Motorhome Park

Located behind cafe at 45 Meander Valley Road. Suitable for self-contained units only. Sullage dump.

GPS S:41 31.567 E:146 50.733

MR: Map 3 C8

FURTHER INFORMATION

Andy's Bakery Cafe

Tel: 03 6393 1846

Web: www.andystasmania.com

Sullage dump fee: From $5.00.

Tree carvings at Legerwood

The South-East and Bruny Island

STRETCHING TO THE NORTH AND south of Hobart, the state's capital city, Tasmania's scenic South-East is a haven for water-based activities with opportunities to explore delightful destinations such as Bruny Island, the Tasman Peninsula and the stunning Freycinet National Park.

BEST CAMPSITES!

- **Richardsons Beach tent-based camping area**
  Freycinet National Park
- **Fortescue Bay Campground**
  Tasman National Park
- **Cloudy Bay Corner Beach campground**
  South Bruny National Park
- **Lime Bay camping area**
  Lime Bay State Reserve
- **Mayfield Bay camping area**
  Mayfield Bay Conservation Area

Separated from the mainland by D'Entrecasteaux Channel, Bruny Island, which is accessed via a vehicular ferry service from Kettering, offers a number of camping areas as well as a range of other activities, including boating, which is popular here.

Lying to the east of Hobart is the Tasman Peninsula, the site of convict-built Port Arthur settlement as well as historic Lime Bay State Reserve, also a reminder of convict times. Tasman National Park, which takes in the south-east corner of the peninsula has vehicle-based and walk-in camping areas.

In the north is one of the region's more popular parks, Freycinet National Park. This spectacular park is well visited during the summer months and has a range of camping areas which are ideal to base yourself while exploring the park via its many walking trails. One walk not to be missed in the park is to the picturesque Wineglass Bay. Also in this area is Maria Island, located offshore from Orford and reached via a ferry from Triabunna. It was at one time a penal settlement but is now a national park offering camping.

Spring, summer and autumn are without doubt the best times to experience this region.

Bicheno
Campbell Town
Highway
36
42
Ross
40
31
Lake
Highway
Swansea
Coles Bay
31
39
41
Oatlands
Midland
Bothwell
Highway
Tasman
Triabunna
Kempton
35
Colebrook
Hamilton
Lyell
Orford
Buckland
38
Campania
Pontville
Bridgewater
Richmond
New Norfolk
Highway
Sorell
33
HOBART
Dunalley
Lauderdale
37
Highway
Huonville
Eaglehawk Neck
Snug
Franklin
Nubeena
34
Geeveston
30
Cygnet
Port Arthur
Tasman Peninsula
44
32
29
Dover
Alonnah
Adventure Bay
Huon
Bruny Island
Southport
43
43
Cockle Creek
29 Bruny Island Neck Game Reserve
30 Cygnet
31 Freycinet National Park
32 Gordon
33 Hobart
34 Huon Valley
35 Kempton
36 Lake Leake
37 Lime Bay State Reserve
38 Maria Island National Park
39 Mayfield Bay Conservation Area
40 Moulting Lagoon Game Reserve
41 Oatlands
42 Ross
43 South Bruny National Park
44 Tasman National Park
N
0
50Km

29 Bruny Island Neck Game Reserve

Bruny Island Neck Game Reserve is located just to the south of the neck which joins North and South Bruny Islands. Signposted access off the B66 road leads to the campsite behind the beach. Limited caravan access. Access to the island is via the ferry service from Kettering.

The Neck camping area

Located on Lutregala Road. Signposted access off the B66 main road, 27.1km south of the ferry terminal and 3.2km north of the B66 and C630 junction. Bring drinking water and firewood.

GPS S:43 17.583 E:147 19.620

MR: Map 11 E5

FURTHER INFORMATION

Parks & Wildlife Service
Bruny Island
Tel: 03 6293 1419
Parks Pass: Not required.
Camping fees: From $10.00 per site/night up to 2 people.

30 Cygnet

Originally named Port de Cygnet Noir (Black Swanport) due to the number of swans in the bay, today Cygnet is a fruit and wine growing area. Located in the heart of the village, the holiday park is a convenient location from where you can take a stroll along one of the area's beaches, visit The Tahune Devil Park or take a drive to Pelverata Falls. Cygnet is on the B68 road, 18km south of Huonville.

Cygnet Holiday Park

Located on Mary Street in Cygnet behind the RSL club and in front of the recreation ground. Access is signposted off the highway. Camp kitchen, laundry.

GPS S:43 09.371 E:147 04.486

MR: Map 11 D4

FURTHER INFORMATION

Cygnet Holiday Park

Tel: 0418 532 160

Web: www.business.google.com/website/cygnet-caravan-park

Camping fees: Unpowered from $12.00 per person/night. Powered from $30.00 per site/night for 2 people.

THE SOUTH-EAST AND BRUNY ISLAND

31 Freycinet National Park

Freycinet National Park is one of Tasmania's most popular coastal destinations. The park offers visitors a range of recreational activities including swimming, snorkelling, beach fishing, scenic drives and a variety of walking tracks to explore. There is magnificent scenery of mountain ranges and beautiful white sandy beaches with clear blue waters. Access to the park is via the Coles Bay Road (C302) off the A3 highway, 11km south of Bicheno. The park's visitor information centre is 1.4km south of Coles Bay.

Richardsons Beach campground - powered sites 1 to 18

Access is 300m north of the park visitor information centre along Freycinet Drive. Camping area for camper trailers, caravans, motorhomes and campervans. Powered sites. Gas/fuel stove only.

GPS S:42 07.446 E:148 17.781

MR: Map 8 J5

Richardsons Beach - The Sand Dunes - tent-based camping area - sites 19 to 45

Access on Freycinet Drive just south of the park visitor information centre. Tent-based camping only. Gas/fuel stove only.

GPS S:42 07.583 E:148 17.965

MR: Map 8 J5

Honeymoon Bay camping area

Signposted access on Freycinet Drive, 1.6km south of the park visitor information centre. Tent-based camping only. Gas/fuel stove only. Open Summer and Easter only.

GPS S:42 08.228 E:148 17.948

MR: Map 8 J5

TO A3 / TASMAN HIGHWAY
Rogers Hill
Friendly Beaches
MOULTING LAGOON GAME RESERVE
FREYCINET NATIONAL PARK
Friendly Beaches
Middle Bank
Moulting Lagoon
Mount Peter
Mount Paul
Friendly Point
TASMAN SEA
Coles Bay Road
Swan River
River & Rocks
FREYCINET NATIONAL PARK
COLES BAY CONSERVATION AREA
Swanwick
Whitewater Wall
Mount Stacey
Hepburn Point
Richardsons Beach (van)
Cape Tourville
Coles Bay
Richardsons Beach (tent)
Coles Bay
Honeymoon Bay
The Fisheries
Mount Dove
The Hazards
Thouin Bay
Fleurieu Point
Wineglass Bay
Great Oyster Bay
Wineglass Bay
Cape Forestier
Promise Bay
Hazards Lagoon
Hazards Beach
Freycinet Peninsula
Mount Graham
Mount Freycinet
Cooks Beach
Gates Bluff
Weatherhead Point
FREYCINET NATIONAL PARK
N
Baldys Bluff
0
5Km

Friendly Beaches camping area

Signposted access along the Coles Bay Road (C302), 8.6km south of the A3 highway. Then 3.9km east into camping area along unsealed road. Individual sites among coastal vegetation above beach. Limited sites suitable for campervans. Bring drinking water. Gas/fuel stove only.

GPS S:41 59.488 E:148 17.205
MR: Map 8 J4

Whitewater Wall camping area

Access track is 2.1km along Cape Tourville Road, which is 1.6km south of the park visitor information centre. Then 2.1km into the small sheltered camping area. Gas/fuel stove only.

GPS S:42 06.297 E:148 20.309
MR: Map 8 J4

Walk-in campsites: Wineglass Bay, Hazards Beach and Cooks Beach

Walk-in bush campsites within the park for overnight self-sufficient walkers. Carry large scale maps. Gas/fuel stove only. Contact Ranger for details of water availability. Walkers must register and deregister at the information/self-registration station in the main car park.

FURTHER INFORMATION

Parks & Wildlife Service Freycinet Visitors Centre

Tel: 03 6256 7000. Ballot system for Christmas holiday period applies, entries in by July 31. Campground bookings are taken for December 19 to February 10 and for Easter only. Outside of these times fees payable at visitor information centre or self-registration stations.
Parks Pass: Required.
Camping fees: From $13.00 per site/night for 2 people.

Friendly Beaches camping area

32 Gordon

Gordon is a small locality on the waters of the D'Entrecasteaux Channel. Access to Gordon is along the B68 road, which is signposted off the A6 highway at Kingston, 11km south of Hobart or from Huonville, 35km south-west of Hobart.

Gordon Oval Reserve

Located on Channel Highway in Gordon. Overnight camping area at the Gordon Oval, camp only in the designated area. Located close to the Gordon Jetty where the boat ramp is located. Bring drinking water.

MR: Map 11 E4

FURTHER INFORMATION

Kingborough Council
Tel: 03 6211 8200
Web: www.kingborough.tas.gov.au
Huon Valley Visitor Centre
Tel: 03 6264 0326
Web: www.huonvalleyvisitorcentre.com.au
Camping fees: From $5.00 per site/night. Payable at on-site honesty box.
Maximum stay: 24 hours.

33 Hobart

The state's capital city is situated on the Derwent River at the foot of the majestic Mount Wellington. This historic harbour city offers a range of activities for the visitor. Visit Risdon Cove; Salamanca Place; Constitution Dock; the Cascade Brewery, museums and art galleries; view historic buildings (there's over ninety buildings in Hobart classified by the National Trust); take a cruise along the river or join a tour of the Cadbury chocolate factory.

Hobart Showground Motorhome Park

Signposted access on Howard Road, which is signposted off the Brooker Highway in Glenorchy, north of Hobart city centre. Camping approved for fully self-contained caravans, motorhomes and campervans ie: units must have own fresh water storage, sealed grey water holding tank, sealed black water holding tank. Camping permit issued from administration office on arrival or at self-registration station outside business hours.

GPS S:42 50.033 E:147 17.100
MR: Map 11 E2

FURTHER INFORMATION

Royal Hobart Showground
Tel: 03 6272 6812
Web: www.hobartshowground.com.au
Camping fees: Tent sites from $25.00 per site/night. Powered site from $29.00 per site/night.
Maximum stay: 14 nights. No camping available during October.

Cascade Brewery, Hobart

34 Huon Valley

Located to the south-west of Hobart, the area is renowned for fresh produce including apples and seafood as well as locally made wines. Nature lovers will enjoy the pristine rivers, caves and beautiful national parks. The Huon Valley Council provides camping and caravan areas in the towns of Franklin and Port Huon.

Franklin Foreshore camping & caravan area

Signposted access on the A6 highway in Franklin. No open fires on ground, bring own fire drum/pot and firewood. Camping permit issued when fees are collected.

GPS S:43 05.499 E:147 00.592

MR: Map 11 C3

FURTHER INFORMATION

Huon Valley Visitor Centre

Tel: 03 6264 0326

Web: www.huonvalleyvisitorcentre.com.au

Camping fees: From $10.00 per site/night. Fees collected daily.

Maximum stay: 4 nights.

DISCOVERER

Franklin Foreshore camping and caravan area, Huon Valley

Shipwrights Point Regatta Ground/Recreation Reserve

Signposted access on the A6 highway at northern end of Port Huon. Camping permit issued when fees are collected.

GPS S:43 09.5100 E:146 58.759

MR: Map C4

FURTHER INFORMATION

Huon Valley Visitor Centre

Tel: 03 6264 0326

Web: www.huonvalleyvisitorcentre.com.au

Camping fees: From $10.00 per site/night. Fees collected daily.

Maximum stay: 4 nights.

Shipwrights Point Regatta Ground/Recreation Reserve

CAMPING WITH YOURDOG

If you own a well behaved and well socialised dog you may wish to take your 'best friend' along camping with you. Dogs are usually welcome in state forests and some reserves, but are not permitted in national parks. Each listing in this guide indicates whether you can bring your dog with you.

35 Kempton

The village of Kempton is located on the Midland Highway, approximately 50km north of Hobart. The town has many historical buildings.

Kempton overnight bay

Located behind 'The Blue Place' on Main Street in Kempton. Access road is diagonally opposite council chambers.

GPS S:42 31.917 E:147 12.133

MR: Map 7 D7

FURTHER INFORMATION

Southern Midlands Council

Tel: 03 6259 3011

Camping fee: From $10.00 per vehicle/night, or free for self-contained units that do not use facilities. Refundable key deposit required for facilities key. There is an on-site donation box for the local Green Ponds Progress Association who maintain the site. Collect facilities key and pay fees to Southern Midlands Council, Main Street Kempton during week days between 8.30am and 4.30pm.

Maximum stay: 2 nights.

Gray water dump station located at rear of Victoria Hall in town.

36 Lake Leake

Lake Leake is located 4km north of the B34 Road between Campbell Town and Swansea. It's a popular spot with anglers chasing trout.

Lake Leake camping area

Located 3.6km north of the B34 highway. Access is signposted off the B34, 28.5km west of the A3 highway and 34km east of Campbell Town. Unsealed access road. Small area. Bring drinking water and firewood.

GPS S:42 00.526 E:147 47.854

MR: Map 8 G4

FURTHER INFORMATION

Lake Leake Caretaker

Tel: 03 6381 1319

Camping fees: Unpowered from $10.50 per site/night for 2 people. Powered from $21.00 per site/night for 2 people.

NB: There are no credit card or Eftpos facilities, cash only payments.

37 Lime Bay State Reserve

The reserve is situated on the Tasman Peninsula north of Premaydena. Colourful wildflowers are abundant during summer and the beaches at Lime Bay offer enjoyable walking. Visit the ruins of the convict station at nearby Coal Mines Historic Site. Access is signposted from Premaydena, which is 9.3km west of Taranna via the B37 off the Arthur Highway (A9).

Lime Bay camping area

Located 18km north of Premaydena at the end of the Coal Mines Road. From Premaydena follow the C341 signposted to Coal Mines Historic Site which is 11.9km north-west of Premaydena. Continue past the historic site for a further 6.6km to the shaded camping area on the waterfront. Suitable for big rigs. Bring drinking water and firewood. Gas/fuel stove preferred.

GPS S:42 57.419 E:147 42.259

MR: Map 12 G2

FURTHER INFORMATION

Parks & Wildlife Service Tasman Peninsula

Tel: 03 6250 3980

Parks Pass: Not required.

Camping fees: From $13.00 per site/night for 2 people. Fees payable at on-site self-registration station.

38 Maria Island National Park

Maria Island was named by Abel Tasman in 1642, in honour of Maria Van Diemen, the wife of the governor of Batavia. The island's history includes a long-time association with local Aboriginal tribes who once canoed across to the island, and with European settlement when the island became a penal settlement in the early 1820s. Escaping convicts would swim or use rafts to return to mainland Tasmania. The penal settlement was abandoned around 1832 and the island's convicts were then housed at Port Arthur. Nowadays, visitors can visit the historic ruins of the convict days and discover the island's past agricultural pursuits. Take in the beautiful bays, rugged cliffs, enjoy one of the many walking tracks, take a bike ride along the island's roads and view an array of birds and wildlife. Access to Maria Island is via a 30-minute ferry trip from Triabunna wharf. Triabunna is signposted along the Tasman Highway (A3 road), 57km north of Sorell and 50km south of Swansea.

Triabunna

Darlington camping area

Located in Darlington, 200 metres from ferry jetty. Coin-operated hot showers. Laundry facilities. Some firewood supplied. Gas/fuel stove preferred.

MR: Map 8 I8

Frenchs Farm camping area

Located 11km south of Darlington. Access is signposted. Gas/fuel stove only.

MR: Map 8 I8

Encampment Cove camping area

Located 13km south of Darlington. Access is signposted. Firewood supplied. Gas/fuel stove preferred.

MR: Map 8 I8

FURTHER INFORMATION

Parks & Wildlife Service Maria Island
Tel: 03 6257 1420
Parks Pass: Required.
Camping fees: From $13.00 per site/night for 2 people. Fees payable at Commissariat Store.
Ferry service: Encounter Maria Island
Tel: 03 62564772. Reservations essential.
Web: www.encountermaria.com.au

39 Mayfield Bay Conservation Area

Mayfield Bay Conservation Area is signposted along the Tasman Highway, 15km south of Swansea and 13km north of Little Swanport. The beaches at Mayfield Bay offer diving, swimming and fishing. Take the short walk to Three Arch Bridge, built in 1845 by convicts.

Mayfield Bay camping area

Signposted access on the Tasman Highway (A3), 15km south of Swansea. Beach boat launch. Bring drinking water and firewood.

GPS S:42 14.406 E:148 00.758
MR: Map 8 I5

FURTHER INFORMATION

Parks & Wildlife Service Freycinet
Tel: 03 6256 7000
Parks Pass: Not required.
Camping fees: Donation, payable at on-site donation box.
NB: Wood collection is not permitted in this area.

40 Moulting Lagoon Game Reserve

Game reserve on shores of Moulting Lagoon. Access is along the Coles Bay Road, south of the Freycinet National Park Friendly Beaches access road.

Middle Bank camping area

Access track is off Coles Bay Road, 3.6km south of the Friendly Beaches Road. Then 200m west into the small camping area, best suited for tent-based camping and self-sufficient campers. Recommended to bring own portable toilet. Bring drinking water and firewood. **NB:** Pets are not permitted at this site.

GPS S:42 01.563 E:148 13.453
MR: Map 8 J4

River and Rocks camping area

Signposted access off Coles Bay Road, 6.9km south of the Middle Bank access track and 7.4km north of Coles Bay. Then 400m west into the well-shaded and popular camping area. Bring drinking water and firewood. **NB:** Dog regulations may change in the future.

GPS S:42 05.198 E:148 13.910
MR: Map 8 J4

FURTHER INFORMATION

Parks & Wildlife Service Freycinet
Tel: 03 6256 7000
Parks Pass: Not required.

River and Rocks camping area

41 Oatlands

The village of Oatlands is located on the Midland Highway, 86km south of Ross and 90km north of Hobart. Numerous historic buildings, antique stores, cafes and a Historical Centre. A walk around the lake is accessible to wheelchairs.

Lake Dulverton camping area

Signposted access along The Esplande in Oatlands. Suitable for self contained units only. Public phone nearby in town.

GPS S:42 18.050 E:147 22.567
MR: Map 7 E6

FURTHER INFORMATION

Southern Midlands Council
Tel: 03 6254 5000
Web: www.southernmidlands.tas.gov.au
Maximum stay: 72 hours.

42 Ross

The picturesque village of Ross is accessed off the Midland Highway. The town's historic buildings date back to the early and mid 1800s. The locally produced information guide has details of these buildings and other attractions, see the Visitor Information Centre on arrival.

Ross Caravan Park

Accessed via High Street in Ross and located adjacent to the Macquarie River. Signposted access. Laundry facilities. Located close to town, walk to all town attractions and facilities.

GPS S:42 01.795 E:147 29.454
MR: Map 7 F4

FURTHER INFORMATION

Ross Caravan Park
Tel: 0437 425 832
Camping fees: Unpowered from $25.00 per site/night for 2 people. Powered from $32.00 per site/night for 2 people.

43 South Bruny National Park

Situated at the southern tip of South Bruny Island, the park covers coastline areas with magnificent scenery, abundant wildlife and some rare vegetation. Access to the island is via the vehicular ferry from Kettering.

Jetty Beach camping area

Signposted access 17km south of Lunawanna along Cape Bruny Road (C629). Then drive in 2.3km to the camping area with dispersed sites among coastal vegetation. Access track is a narrow, single lane track. Beach boat launch. Bring drinking water and firewood. Gas/fuel stove preferred.

GPS S:43 27.580 E:147 09.157

MR: Map 11 D6

The Pines camping area

Signposted access 9km south of Lunawanna along Cloudy Bay Road (C644). Then drive in 600m to the small camping area in grove of pines. Bring drinking water and firewood. Gas/fuel stove preferred.

GPS S:43 26.246 E:147 14.807

MR: Map 11 E6

Woodbridge Hill
Nicholls Rivulet
Woodbridge
Highway
Creek
Roberts Point
Apollo Bay
Roberts Hill
Missionary Hills
Bruny Island
Trumpeter Bay
Heeneys Bluff
Gardners Bay
Birchs Bay
Soldiers Point
Missionary Bay
Adams Bay
Dears Ridge
Mount Cygnet
Island
Channel
Port Cygnet
Flowerpot
Great Bay
Variety Bay
Variety Point
Clennett Hills
Buxtons Hill
Chuckle Head
Church Hill
Majors Hill
Garden
BRUNY ISLAND NECK GAME RESERVE
Fancy Bay
Middleton
Simpsons Point
Garden Island Creek
Garden Island Sands
Isthmus Bay
Moorina Bay
Mount Grosse
Gordon
Cape Queen Elizabeth
Highway
D'Entrecasteaux Channel
Verona Sands
Neck Beach
Simpsons Bay
Ninepin Point
Huon Point
Sheepwash Bay
Driscolls Hill
The Neck
Alonnah
Adventure Bay
Coal Point
Ventenat Point
Mount Bounty
Grass Point
SOUTH BRUNY NATIONAL PARK
Adventure Bay
Little Taylors Bay
Lunawanna
Cookville
Fluted Cape
Ventenat Hill
Mount Mangana
South Bruny Range
Stafford Hill
Road
Partridge Island
Mount Tobin
Mount Cook
Cape Connella
Bruny Island
Tinpot Point
Cloudy
Mount Midway
Bay of Islands
Cloudy Bay Lagoon
Mount Bleak
Great Taylors Bay
Lighthouse
Labillardiere Peninsula
The Pines
Mangana Bluff
Jetty Beach
Cloudy Bay
Standaway Bay
SOUTH BRUNY NATIONAL PARK
Mabel Bay
Cloudy Bay Beach Corner
TASMAN SEA
Mount Barren
Mount Bruny
Lighthouse Bay
SOUTH BRUNY NATIONAL PARK
Cape Bruny
West Cloudy Head
East Cloudy Head
Pyramid Bay
Boreel Head
Tasman Head
N
0
10Km

Cloudy Bay Corner Beach campground

4WD beach access, 9.9km south of Lunawanna at end of Cloudy Bay Road (C644). Camping area is located 3km from beach entrance track via Cloudy Bay Beach. Check tide times prior to driving on the beach. Unpatrolled beach, be aware of rips when swimming. Popular surfing beach. Beach boat launch. Bring drinking water and firewood. Gas/fuel stove preferred.

GPS S:43 28.090 E:147 14.967
MR: Map 11 E6

FURTHER INFORMATION

Parks & Wildlife Service Bruny Island
Tel: 03 6293 1419
Parks Pass: Required.
Camping fees: From $10.00 per site/night for 2 people

44 Tasman National Park

Along with the beautiful coastal scenery, Tasman National Park also offers visitors bushwalking, swimming and fishing opportunities. Signposted access to the park's campground at Fortescue Bay is off the Arthur Highway (A9). Access the north of the park via the Blowhole Road (C338).

TASMAN NATIONAL PARK WALK-IN CAMPSITES

Bivouac Bay campsite

Walk-in bush campsite along the Tasman Trail, north of Fortescue Bay. Trail can be accessed from Fortescue Bay Campground or from the north from Waterfall Bay Road. Gas/fuel stove only. Carry drinking water and maps.

MR: Map 12 H3

Camp Falls campsite

Walk-in bush campsite along the Tasman Trail, south of Waterfall Bay carpark. Trail can be accessed from Waterfall Bay Road or from the south from Fortescue Bay Campground. Gas/fuel stove only. Carry drinking water and maps.

MR: Map 12 H3

FURTHER INFORMATION

Parks & Wildlife Tasman Peninsula
Tel: 03 6250 3980
Parks Pass: Required.

Fortescue Bay Campground

Signposted access along the A9 highway, 3.4km south of the A9/B37 junction and 4km north of Port Arthur. Then drive in south-easterly direction for 12.2km to large camping area situated around the bay with 41 sites. Limited sites for big rigs. Hot showers operated by tokens, available for purchase from office. Boil drinking water. Bring firewood or purchase on site.

GPS S:43 08.512 E:147 57.810

MR: Map 12 H4

FURTHER INFORMATION

Fortescue Bay Campground

Tel: 03 6250 2433. Bookings necessary.

Parks Pass: Required.

Camping fees: From $13.00 per site/night for 2 people. Fees payable to caretaker at Fortescue Bay office.

The South-West Wilderness

THE SOUTH-WEST IS A VAST TRACT OF rugged and spectacular wilderness with few roads, although a number of camping opportunities exist at some picturesque locations around the fringe of this huge forested area. Much of this region is protected by the Southwest National Park, which has a selection of vehicle-based campsites and is also traversed by a number of multi-day walking trails. The famed lakes of Pedder and Gordon sit in the centre of the region and are surrounded by the park. A haven for anglers and bushwalkers, access to this World Heritage area is via Westerway. En route visitors can enjoy the nearby Mt Field National Park, which along with delightful Russell Falls also offers a number of walking trails as well the popular Land of Giants camping area.

Well-visited locations in the southern part of the region are around Recherche Bay where there are some delightful camping areas bordering the Southwest National Park at Cockle Creek, as well as in the park itself at Boltons Green.

To the north and inland from the timber town of Geeveston is the Tahune AirWalk. Here visitors can stroll amongst the treetops, looking out over the Huon River. There are a number of forest drives in the area, with some routes providing access to secluded campsites.

On the west coast camping is possible at Macquarie Heads near Strahan while experienced walkers can camp along the walking track to Frenchmans Cap.

The preferred time for camping and walking in this region is late spring, summer and early autumn, especially the inland lakes and coastal walks.

BEST CAMPSITES!

- **Edgar Campground**
  Southwest National Park
- **Land of the Giants Campground**
  Mt Field National Park
- **Cockle Creek Campground**
  Recherche Bay Nature Recreation Area
- **Boltons Green Campground**
  Southwest National Park
- **Esperance camping site**
  Southern Forests

45 Bothwell
46 Bradys Lake
47 Bronte Lagoon
48 Franklin-Gordon Wild Rivers National Park
49 Hartz Mountains National Park
50 Lake Binney
51 Lake Burbury
52 Lake King William
53 Lake Meadowbank
54 Laughing Jack Lagoon
55 Lune River
56 Macquarie Heads
57 Mt Field National Park
58 Recherche Bay Nature Recreation Area
59 Repulse State Forest
60 Southern Forests
61 Southwest National Park
62 Tahune Forest Reserve
63 Wayatinah Lagoon

45 Bothwell

Founded by the Scots in 1824, the village of Bothwell has over 50 buildings, built mainly by convict labour, that are classified or recognised by the National Trust. As well the village is home to Australia's oldest golf course. Bothwell is situated on the A5 Highway, 76km north of Hobart.

Bothwell Camping Ground

Located in Market Place, Bothwell. Gas/fuel stove only. Key access to showers. Laundry facilities.

GPS S:42 22.967 E:147 00.483

MR: Map 7 C6

FURTHER INFORMATION

Central Highlands Council

Tel: 03 6259 5503

Web: www.centralhighlands.tas.gov.au

Bothwell Garage

Tel: 03 6259 5599

Camping fees: Unpowered from $21.00 per site/night. Powered from $26.00 per site/night. Fees payable and keys available at council office, Alexander Street, Bothwell during hours of Mon to Fri 9am to 4.30pm, or from Bothwell Garage outside of these hours.

46 Bradys Lake

Bradys Lake is popular with fisherfolk and watersports enthusiasts. Access to the lake is signposted along the A10 highway south of the A10 and B11 highways junction.

Bradys Lake camping area

Signposted access off the A10 highway, 6.3km south of the A10 and B11 highways junction. There are two access tracks, one south of the canal and one north of the canal, which lead into dispersed bush camping beside the lake. Suitable for big rigs. Use of portable toilets recommended. Bring drinking water and firewood. Gas/stove preferred.

GPS S:42 14.043 E:146 29.708

MR: Map 7 A5

FURTHER INFORMATION

Hydro Tasmania

Tel: 1300 360 441

Web: www.hydro.com.au

Maximum stay: 7 days.

47 Bronte Lagoon

Bronte Lagoon is located to the west of the A10 highway. Access is signposted off the A10 highway 200m south-east of its junction with the B11 highway. The lagoon is a popular fishing and boating destination.

Bronte Lagoon camping area

Signposted access off the A10 highway, 200m south of its junction with the B11 highway. Then travel in 2km to boat ramp and campsites, or cross the dam wall and travel for a further 400m to more sites. Camp only in designated areas. No facilities, suitable for self-sufficient campers only. Use of portable toilets recommended. Bring drinking water and firewood. Gas/stove preferred.

GPS S:42 11.197 E:146 28.768

MR: Map 7 A5

FURTHER INFORMATION

Hydro Tasmania

Tel: 1300 360 441

Web: www.hydro.com.au

Maximum stay: 7 days.

48 Franklin-Gordon Wild Rivers National Park

Protecting the Franklin, Gordon, Jane and Denison rivers, Franklin-Gordon Wild Rivers National Park is part of the Tasmanian Wilderness World Heritage Area. The majority of the park is rugged and remote, however there are numerous stop-offs along the Lyell Highway which provide access to the park's natural sites including magnificent rainforests, the scenic Nelson Falls, the wild Franklin and Collingwood Rivers. There are spectacular views from Donaghys Hill Wilderness Lookout. For more experienced walkers there is the multi-day Frenchmans Cap Track which leads to the summit of the 1443-metre Frenchmans Cap.

Nelson Falls

Frenchmans Cap Track camping areas

Frenchmans Cap walkers must register and deregister at trackhead. Carry large scale maps. Contact ranger for further details. Walkers must be prepared for dramatic weather changes. Experienced self-sufficient walkers with high level of fitness only. Trackhead and walker registration signposted along the Lyell Highway, 3km west of the Franklin River Bridge, 30km west of Derwent Bridge and 40km east of Queenstown. Gas/fuel stove only.

Trackhead **GPS** S:42 12.507 E:145 58.856
MR: Map 6 J5
Loddon River and Philps Creek: No facilities prior to Lake Vera.
Lake Vera: 16km from trackhead. Hut with coal heater, coal supplied.
Lake Tahune: 9km from Lake Vera. Hut with metho heater, limited metho supplied. Carry own.
Frenchmans Cap: 1km from Lake Tahune. No camping.

FURTHER INFORMATION

Parks & Wildlife Service Queenstown
Tel: 03 6471 2511
Parks Pass: Required.

Hartz Mountains National Park

49 Hartz Mountains National Park

Hartz Mountains National Park offers magnificent views across to the southern coast and over remote mountain ranges. The park has a variety of landscapes including waterfalls and highland lakes, formed during past ice ages by glaciers. The diverse landscapes provide habitat for rainforest, alpine heath and eucalypt forests. Walk to one of the glacial lakes or to the higher ranges for panoramic views. Hartz Peak is the highest peak in the park at 1255m. Access to Hartz Mountains National Park is signposted along the C632 road 13km west of Geeveston, then travel 13.5km south to the car park and picnic area. Visitors need to be aware of and prepared for extreme weather changes.

Hartz Mountains bush camping

Walk-in bush camping is allowed within the park as per Parks and Wildlife bush camping regulations (must be 500m from any road or day use area). Self-sufficient walkers only. Bring drinking water. Gas/fuel stove only.

Car park **GPS** S:43 13.039 E:146 46.234
Car park **MR:** Map 11 B4

FURTHER INFORMATION

Parks & Wildlife Service Huonville
Tel: 03 6121 7026
Parks Pass: Required.
All walkers must register and de-register at information booth within the park. Walkers need to carry large scale maps, contact ranger for further details.

50 Lake Binney

This large lake is situated beside the A10 highway and provides fishing and boating opportunities. Access to Lake Binney's main boat ramp is signposted off the A10 highway, 3km south of Bradys Lake.

Lake Binney camping area

Signposted access off the A10 highway, 3km south of Bradys Lake. A small bush camping area is located beside the highway near the boat ramp. Further bush campsites are located on the lake's eastern shore and can be accessed off the road that crosses the dam wall. Use of portable toilets recommended. Bring drinking water and firewood. Gas/fuel stove preferred.

GPS S:42 15.321 E:146 28.679
MR: Map 7 A5

FURTHER INFORMATION

Hydro Tasmania
Tel: 1300 360 441
Web: www.hydro.com.au
Maximum stay: 7 days.

Duckhole Lake Walk, Southern Forests

51 Lake Burbury

Lake Burbury is a large water storage area of 54 square kilometers to the north and south of the A10 highway and situated east of Queenstown. The waters from Lake Burbury travel for seven kilometers through a tunnel to the John Butters Power Station on the banks of the King River. Access to the lake is signposted along the A10 highway east of Queenstown and provides boating and fishing opportunities.

Lake Burbury camping area

Signposted access along the A10 highway, 20.7km east of Queenstown and 86km west of Derwent Bridge. Then drive in 700m to large camping area with limited shade. Suitable for big rigs. Gas/fuel stove only.

GPS S:42 05.808 E:145 40.490

MR: Map 6 H4

FURTHER INFORMATION

Lake Burbury Camping Area Caretaker

Tel: 03 6471 2762. Telephone contact available after 5.30pm.

Camping fees: Contact caretaker for current rates. Fees payable to caretaker.

Thureau Hills camping area

Signposted access to boat ramp and camping area along the A10 highway, 15km east of Queenstown. Then drive 3.6km south to the camping area, which has limited tent-based camping and is best suited for camper trailers, caravans, motorhomes and campervans. Suitable for big rigs. Bring drinking water and firewood.

GPS S:42 08.634 E:145 39.026
MR: Map 6 H5

FURTHER INFORMATION

West Coast Council, Queenstown
Tel: 03 6471 5880

Thureau Hills camping area

COLLECTING FIREWOOD

Most camping areas, especially the more popular ones, are usually devoid of any firewood. If firewood is not supplied by the land managers, it's best to collect enough wood for your needs well before getting to your campsite, or to bring some from home. Please do not cut down any trees, either living or dead, from around the camping area.

52 Lake King William

Lake King William is a water storage area situated to the west of Derwent Bridge, and is part of the Derwent Catchment to supply water to the Tarraleah Power Station. The lake is a popular angling site for trout and is accessed off the A10 highway.

Lake King William bush camping

Access tracks to Lake King William are off the A10 highway, 1.7km and 3.7km south of Derwent Bridge Hotel. The northern access track, 1.7km south of Derwent Bridge, leads in 100m to bush campsites around the top of the lake. The southern access track, 3.7km south of Derwent Bridge, leads in 900m to a boat ramp with bush camping in the vicinity. Note: limited motorhome and campervan access to this southern area due to narrow access track with some overhanging vegetation. Bring drinking water. Gas/fuel stove preferred.

Northern sites **GPS** S:42 08.842 E:146 13.074
Southern sites **GPS** S:42 09.522 E:146 12.964
MR: Map 6 K5

FURTHER INFORMATION

Hydro Tasmania
Tel: 1300 360 441
Web: www.hydro.com.au
Maximum stay: 7 days.

53 Lake Meadowbank

Lake Meadowbank is another of the water storage areas within the Derwent Catchment which includes 16 dams and 10 power stations, along with a number of canals, tunnels, weirs and pipelines. Access to the lake is along the Dunrobin Bridge Road, which is signposted along the A10 highway, 7km south of Ouse and 7km north-west of Hamilton. The lake is popular for fishing, canoeing, swimming, water-skiing and boating.

Bethune Park camping area

Access signposted through gate, 2km west of the A10 highway along the Dunrobin Bridge Road (Ellendale Road/ C608 road), at the western end of the bridge. Grassed area on the western foreshore of the lake, suitable for big rigs in the top parking area. Boat ramp on lake's eastern shore. Bring drinking water and firewood. Gas/fuel stove preferred.

GPS S:42 32.180 E:146 43.824
MR: Map 7 B7

FURTHER INFORMATION

Hydro Tasmania
Tel: 1300 360 441
Web: www.hydro.com.au
Maximum stay: 7 days.

54 Laughing Jack Lagoon

This interestingly named lagoon is a storage area within the Derwent Catchment. Access to Laughing Jack Lagoon is signposted on the A10 highway, 20km east of Derwent Bridge via the C602 road, and is a favoured fishing destination.

Laughing Jack Lagoon bush camping

Signposted access along the A10 highway, 20km east of Derwent Bridge and 6.2km west of the B11 highway. From the A10 highway travel south along the C602 road for 2.6km, then turn into the signposted C602 and follow it for 6.8km to dam wall. At dam wall a track on left leads to bush campsites best suited for tents and off-road camper trailers. Track on right at dam wall crosses bridge and leads to further sites. Use of portable toilets recommended. Bring drinking water and firewood. Gas/fuel stove preferred.

GPS S:42 10.614 E:146 19.920
MR: Map 6 K5

FURTHER INFORMATION

Hydro Tasmania
Tel: 1300 360 441
Web: www.hydro.com.au
Maximum stay: 7 days.

Big Tree Reserve, Styx River

55 Lune River

At Lune River is the Ida Bay Railway, the last of the many bush tramways built in Tasmania. The historic 1940s locos and passenger carriages travel along a 7km section of narrow gauge railway to the end of the line at Deep Hole and Elliott's Beach, where there are marked walking tracks and a scenic beach. En route you will view historic sites beside the railway including the original town site of Ida Bay along with scenic forests. Ida Bay Railway is located at Lune River on the C636 road, 7km south of the A6 highway.

Ida Bay Railway camping area

Signposted access along the C636 road 7km south of the A6 highway. Communal cabin with full cooking facilities, heating and lounge area. Laundry facilities and cafe.

GPS S:43 26.605 E:146 54.219

MR: Map 11 C6

FURTHER INFORMATION

Ida Bay Railway

Tel: 03 6298 3110. Bookings preferred.

Web: www.idabayrailway.com.au

Camping fees: From $23.00 per site/night for 2 people.

56 Macquarie Heads

Macquarie Heads is the northern head of the mouth of the Macquarie Harbour. The heads are located 15km south of the historic port town of Strahan. Fishing at the heads is a very popular past time.

Macquarie Harbour, Strahan

Macquarie Heads camping area

Located at the end of the C251 (Macquarie Heads Road), 14km south of Strahan. Access is signposted from Strahan. Unsealed access road, which can be rough at times. Suitable for big rigs. Bring own fire drum/pot and firewood.

GPS S:42 13.213 E:145 14.268

MR: Map 5 F5

FURTHER INFORMATION

Macquarie Heads Caretaker

Tel: 03 6471 7382. Telephone contact available between 5pm and 8pm.

Camping fees: Contact caretaker for current rates.

57 Mt Field National Park

Located just over an hours drive from Hobart, Mt Field National Park is one of Tasmania's oldest national parks. The park protects a diverse range of flora of tall swamp gum forests, rainforests and tree ferns, which in turn provides a habitat to a variety of wildlife including quolls, bandicoots, possums and bettongs. Visitors to Mt Field National Park can enjoy a number of walking trails through magnificent fern forests and to the scenic Russell Falls, or walk or drive to the historic Government Huts in the Lake Dobson area of the park. The park's camping area is situated beside the Tyena River and visited by kangaroos and pademelons during the morning and afternoon. Access to the park is signposted along the C609 road which is signposted off the B61 road at Westerway, 29km north-west of New Norfolk.

Land of the Giants Campground

Signposted access along the Lake Dobson Road (C609), 7.6km west of Westerway, which is situated on the B61 road, 29km north-west of New Norfolk. Then drive in 1km to the large, grassed and shaded camping area, and the national park visitor centre. Suitable for big rigs. Laundry facilities. Gas/fuel stove only.

GPS S:42 41.072 E:146 42.955
MR: Map 7 B8

FURTHER INFORMATION

Parks & Wildlife Service Mt Field
Tel: 03 6288 1149
Parks Pass: Required.
Camping fees: Unpowered from $16.00 per site/night for 2 people. Powered from $20.00 per site/ night for 2 people. Fees payable at self-registration station.

Land of the Giants Campground, Mt Field National Park

58 Recherche Bay Nature Recreation Area

This attractive recreation area is situated close to the southern tip of the island. Recherche Bay Nature Recreation Area looks out over the Recherche Bay and has beautiful coastal scenery, excellent swimming, fishing and beach walks. Access is along the Cockle Creek Road (C636), which is signposted off the A6 highway 3km north of Southport. The first camping area is 21km along the C636 road from the A6.

Gilhams Beach campground

Signposted access along Cockle Creek Road, 14.2km south of the Ida Bay Railway. Suitable for big rigs. Bring drinking water and firewood.

GPS S:43 32.526 E:146 53.532

MR: Map 11 C6

Recherche Bay Nature Recreation Area

Finns Beach campground

Signposted access along Cockle Creek Road, 800m south of Gilhams Beach access track. Suitable for big rigs. Bring drinking water and firewood.

GPS S:43 32.895 E:146 53.263
MR: Map 11 C6

Catamaran River campground

Signposted access along Cockle Creek Road, 1.1km south of Finns Beach access track. Suitable for big rigs. Bring drinking water and firewood.

GPS S:43 33.276 E:146 53.269
MR: Map 11 C6

Cockle Creek campground

Signposted access along Cockle Creek Road, 3km south of Catamaran River campground and north of bridge at Cockle Creek. Suitable for big rigs. Bring drinking water and firewood. **NB:** South side of bridge is Southwest National Park - pets not permitted the national park.

GPS S:43 34.659 E:146 53.214
MR: Map 11 C6

FURTHER INFORMATION

Parks & Wildlife Service Huonville
Tel: 03 6121 7026
Parks Pass: Not required.
Maximum stay: 1 month.

59 Repulse State Forest

Forest area on western foreshore of Lake Repulse. To reach the forest, take the Ellendale Road from the A10 highway which is 6.7km south of Ouse. Then take Dawson Road, which is 2.7km west of the highway. Follow Dawson Road for 11.4km to enter the forest. At this reading there is a track on the right which leads to various tracks to the lake's foreshore and bush campsites.

Lake Repulse bush camping

Numerous tracks lead to bush campsites on lake foreshore within the forest. Steep access tracks. Sites suitable for camper trailers with 4WD tow vehicles. Be aware of logging trucks. Some sites have natural boat launches. Bring drinking water and firewood.

Access track **GPS** S:42 30.340 E:146 37.045
MR: Map 7 A7

FURTHER INFORMATION

Sustainable Timber Tasmania
Derwent Park
Tel: 03 6235 8100

60 Southern Forests

Owing to the high rainfall and rich soils, the Southern Forests comprise mainly of wet eucalypt forests and cloak the valleys of the Weld, Picton, Arve, Huon, Lune and Esperance rivers. Activities include walking, rafting, car touring, fishing and camping.

Esperance camping site

Located 7.7km along Esperance River Road. Esperance River Road is signposted off the A6 highway at Strathblane, which is 4.4km south of the Dover Hotel. Camping on the north side of the Esperance River. Tent-based camping, carry gear from car park into large grassed area with facilities. Vehicle, camper trailer and caravan-based camping at nearby grassed clearings. Water from river, boil first. Some firewood supplied.

GPS S:43 17.950 E:146 54.716
MR: Map 11 C5

Arve River picnic & camping area

Signposted access along Arve Road, 15km west of Geeveston at the Arve River Streamside Reserve. Tent-based camping, carry gear over bollards. Limited space for small camper trailers, caravans and campervans. Water from tank. Some firewood supplied.

GPS S:43 09.515 E:146 48.400
MR: Map 11 B4

FURTHER INFORMATION

Sustainable Timber Tasmania
Geeveston
Tel: 03 6295 7111

Esperance camping site, Southern Forests

61 Southwest National Park

Covering over six hundred thousand hectares of remote wild country, Southwest National Park is Tasmania's largest national park. In the south of the park is Cockle Creek which is the start/finish of the South Coast Track. Other shorter walks can also be enjoyed from here. In the north of the park are the excellent trout fishing lakes of Lake Gordon and Lake Pedder. Visit the Gordon Dam and Hydro visitor centre.

COCKLE CREEK

Boltons Green Campground

Located on Cockle Creek Road on south side of bridge at Cockle Creek, 20km south of Lune River. Suitable for big rigs.

Ranger on site during summer. Bring drinking water. Gas/fuel stove only.

GPS S:43 34.963 E:146 53.701

MR: Map 11 C7

FURTHER INFORMATION

Parks & Wildlife Service Huonville

Tel: 03 6121 7026

Park Pass: Required

Boltons Green Campground

LAKE PEDDER

Edgar Campground

Signposted access 30.3km along Scotts Peak Dam Road (C607), which is signposted off the B61 road. Scotts Peak Dam Road is signposted off the B61 road 43km east of Strathgordon and 50km west of Westerway. Grassed camping area with 10 sites and some shade. Carry insect repellant. Boat ramp located nearby at Scotts Peak Dam.

GPS S:43 01.803 E:146 21.004

MR: Map 10 F3

FURTHER INFORMATION

Hydro Tasmania

Tel: 1300 360 441

Web: www.hydro.com.au

Maximum stay: 7 days.

Huon Campground

Signposted access 6km west of Edgar Campground along the Scotts Peak Dam Road. Then drive in 1km to the small, well-protected camping area with 7 sites. Boat ramp nearby at Scotts Peak Dam. Trackhead for the Port Davey Walking Track. Bring drinking water. Some firewood supplied.

GPS S:43 02.265 E:146 18.087

MR: Map 10 E3

Teds Beach Campground

Signposted access on Strathgordon Road (B61 road), 38km west of Scotts Peak Dam Road and 3km east of Strathgordon. Limited tent-based camping. Gas/fuel stove only.

GPS S:42 47.219 E:146 03.660

MR: Map 10 D1

FURTHER INFORMATION

Parks & Wildlife Service Mt Field
Tel: 03 6288 1149
Parks Pass: Required.

Teds Beach Campground

SOUTHWEST NATIONAL PARK WALKING TRACKS

Port Davey Track camping areas

Walking track from Scotts Peak to Melaleuca, 3-4 days. Trackhead and walkers registration at Huon Campground on Scotts Peak Dam Road (C607) off the B61 Road. Self-sufficient experienced walkers. Gas/fuel stove only.

Trackhead **GPS** S:43 02.265 E:146 18.087
Trackhead **MR:** Map 10 E3
Huon Campground: See page 107.
Junction Creek
Crossing River
Spring River
Bathurst Narrows
Melaleuca: Toilet and walker's huts located here.

South Coast Track camping areas

Walking track from Cockle Creek to Melaleuca, 6-8 days. Trackhead and walkers registration at Cockle Creek on Cockle Creek Road. Self-sufficient experienced walkers. Gas/fuel stove only.

Trackhead **MR:** 11 C7
Cockle Creek: See Boltons Green, page 105.
South Cape Rivulet
Granite Beach (east)
Surprise Bay
New River Lagoon Boat Crossing
Deadman's Bay
Louisa River
Point Eric
Melaleuca: Toilet and walker's huts located here.

FURTHER INFORMATION

Parks & Wildlife Service Huonville
Tel: 03 6121 7026
Parks Pass: Required.
All walkers must register and de-register at registration booths. Walkers need to carry large scale maps, contact ranger for further details and for details of other walking tracks.

62 Tahune Forest Reserve

This beautiful reserve is on the banks of the Huon River and home to the popular Tahune Forest AirWalk. The AirWalk winds through the forest 20 metres above ground level. Huon pines can been seen along the Huon Pine Walk. The Tahune Forest AirWalk and Visitor Centre is located 30km north-west of Geeveston along the Arve Road.

Tahune Forest Reserve camping area

Located adjacent to the Tahune AirWalk car park at the end of Arve Road, 30km north-west of Geeveston. Small camping area with 5 sites suitable only for campervans and motorhomes. All facilities are located at the nearby visitor centre.

GPS S:43 05.684 E:146 43.847
MR: Map 11 B3

FURTHER INFORMATION

Tahune Adventutres
Tel: 03 6251 3903. Campers need to check in at the Visitor Centre's front counter on arrival.
Web: www.tahuneadventures.com.au
Camping fees: One night free with purchase of Tahune Adventure Admission Ticket.

Tahune Forest AirWalk, Tahune Forest Reserve

63 Wayatinah Lagoon

Located north of New Norfolk with signposted access off the Lyell Highway (A10). Wayatinah is home to the six station Lower Derwent hydro-electric scheme. The lagoon offers good trout fishing.

Wayatinah Lakeside Caravan Park

Signposted access along Wayatinah Road in Wayatinah. Wayatinah Road is signposted off the A10 highway, 38km north of Hamilton. Camp kitchen, pool, tennis court and laundry facilities. Bring firewood.

GPS S:42 23.148 E:146 30.330

MR: Map 6 L6

FURTHER INFORMATION

Wayatinah Lakeside Caravan Park

Tel: 03 6289 3317. Bookings essential during school holidays and long weekends.

Web: www.wayatinah.net

Camping fees: Unpowered from $20.00 per site/night for 2 people. Powered from $25.00 per site/2 people

THE SOUTH-WEST WILDERNESS

The Rugged North-West

SITED IN THE PATH OF 'THE ROARING Forties' as they blow in from the Southern Ocean, the rugged North-West of Tasmania offers spectacular coastal scenery, sweeping plains and vast tracts of old-growth forest of the Tarkine. These weather conditions often create ideal surfing conditions, making this region a popular destination for keen board riders and windsurfers. The region also offers some of the best car touring in the state.

BEST CAMPSITES!

- **Manuka Campground**
  Arthur-Pieman Conservation Area
- **Prickly Wattles Campground**
  Arthur-Pieman Conservation Area
- **Black River camping area**
  Peggs Beach Conservation Area
- **O'Neils Creek Reserve**
  Gowrie Park
- **Montagu Camping Ground**
  Montagu Recreation Reserve

The remote and wild Arthur-Pieman Conservation Area runs along the west coast, taking in the Arthur and Pieman rivers, and offers some great camping and fishing. There are a number of campsites here to choose from. In the south is the one-time gold mining settlement of Corinna. Situated on the scenic Pieman River, there are boat cruises available along the river, or if you have your own water transport a boat ramp is located near the ferry. Majestic Huon pines can be seen along the river's edge growing in their natural environs. It's even said that the forests along the river are home to the last of the thylacine!

On the north coast facing Bass Strait are Montague Recreation Reserve and Peggs Beach Conservation Area. Here swimming, fishing and beachcombing can be enjoyed over the warmer months.

Located in the centre of the region is the township of Waratah, once home to one of the world's richest tin mines, while in the east is the delightful town of Sheffield, with its beautiful colourful murals. Both towns offer camping for travellers.

You can enjoy this region year round, however the warmer months of the year tend to be the most popular and are probably the best time to visit as winter can be cold and windy at times.

0
50Km
N
64 Arthur-Pieman Conservation Area
65 Deloraine
66 Gowrie Park
67 Julius River Forest Reserve
68 Lake Barrington
69 Lake Gairdner
70 Lake Mackintosh
71 Latrobe
72 Marrawah
73 Montagu Recreation Reserve
74 Peggs Beach Conservation Area
75 Penguin Area
76 Pieman River State Reserve
77 Port Sorell
78 Railton
79 Riana
80 Sheffield
81 Waratah
82 Wynyard
Montagu
Stanley
Smithton
Bass
Highway
Marrawah
Wynyard
Burnie
Arthur River
Penguin
Port Sorell
Ulverstone
Devonport
Temma
Highway
Sheffield
Railton
ARTHUR PIEMAN CONSERVATION AREA
Waratah
Savage River
Murchison
Highway
Deloraine
Mole Creek
Corinna
Cradle Valley
Rosebery
Zeehan
Zeehan
Highway
CRADLE MOUNTAIN-LAKE ST CLAIR NATIONAL PARK
Miena
Queenstown
Lyell
Derwent Bridge
Strahan
Bronte Park
Tarraleah
FRANKLIN-GORDON WILD RIVERS NATIONAL PARK
Highway
Ouse

64 Arthur-Pieman Conservation Area

Located on the north-west coast. Access is from Smithon via the A2 to Marrawah then travel south along the C214. This large conservation area of 100 000 hectares covers the region between the Arthur River in the north and the Pieman River in the south. Activities include fishing, diving, sea kayaking and surfing.

Manuka Campground

Signposted access along Arthur River Road, 200m north of Arthur River ranger base. Suitable for big rigs. Boil water first. Bring firewood.

GPS S:41 02.721 E:144 40.109

MR: Map 1 C5

Manuka Campground

Ann Bay
Green Point
Green Point
Marrawah
Redpa
Port Hills
Redpa Hill
Hays Tier
Seventeen Mile Plain
Togari
TO SMITHTON
Christmas Hills
Brittons Swamp
Brittons Hill
Rainbow Hill
Bass Highway
Bond Tier
Dismal Swamp
West Point
WEST POINT STATE RESERVE
Mawson Bay
Arthur River Road
ARTHUR PIEMAN CONSERVATION AREA
Seymour Hill
Montagu River
Richardsons Flats
Duffs Flat
Bluff Hill Point
Manuka
Peppermint
Arthur River
Gardiner Point
Prickly Wattles
Arthur
Bullocky Hill
Wuthering Heights Plain
Frankland
Dunns Plain
River
ARTHUR-PIEMAN CONSERVATION AREA
Sundown Point
Nelson Bay
Nelson Bay
Couta Rocks
Rebecca Road
River
Temma
Bullocky Hill
Hazard Bay
Balfour
Mount Balfour
Mount Frankland
SOUTHERN OCEAN
Ordnance Point
TO CORINNA
Mount Hazelton
4WD Only
Kenneth Bay
ARTHUR-PIEMAN CONSERVATION AREA
Mount Lily
West Bluff
Norfolk Range
Sandy Cape
Mount Mabel
Mount Holloway
N
0
10Km
Mount Norfolk
Mount Edith

Peppermint Campground

Signposted access along Arthur River Road in Arthur River village, next to ranger base. Limited trailer and caravan sites, best suited for tent-based camping. Bring drinking water and firewood.

GPS S:41 02.877 E:144 40.055

MR: Map 1 C5

Prickly Wattles Campground

Signposted access along Arthur River Road, 2km south of the Arthur River ranger base. Boil water first. Bring firewood.

GPS S:41 03.550 E:144 40.825

MR: Map 1 C5

Prickly Wattles Campground

Nelson Bay Campground

Signposted access along the C214 road, 10.7km south of Arthur River ranger base. Travel east for 2.3km to road junction. Camping to the right on grassed area. Suitable for self-sufficient campers, as site is near private huts and cabins. Bring drinking water and firewood. Carry own firepot or brazier. Use of portable toilets recommended.

GPS S:41 07.748 E:144 40.330

MR: Map 1 C6

Sandy Cape camping area

Located 50km south of Arthur River and 26km south of Temma. 4WD access only via Temma or via the Balfour Track off the Corinna Road. Well-equipped/experienced 4WD only. Contact Ranger for track conditions and to obtain an Off Road Authority for travel to Sandy Cape. Swimming beach nearby. Bring drinking water and firewood.

GPS S:41 25.667 E:144 45.700

MR: Map 1 C7

Bush camping areas

Walk-in bush camping throughout the park is allowed. Carry large scale maps and contact Parks office for further details. Bring drinking water. Gas/fuel stove preferred.

FURTHER INFORMATION

Parks & Wildlife Service Arthur River
Tel: 03 6457 1225
Parks Pass: Not required.
Camping fees: Manuka and Peppermint CGs from $13.00 per site/night up to 2 adults. Other sites from $6.00 per site/night up to 2 adults. Fees payable at Arthur River ranger base during work hours. Use self-registration box at ranger base after hours.

65 Deloraine

Deloraine is situated at the foothills of the Great Western Tiers on the Meander River, 54km west of Launceston and 50km south-east of Devonport. Classified by the National Trust, there are many beautifully restored Georgian and Victorian buildings in and around the town.

Deloraine Apex Caravan Park

Signposted access along West Parade. Located beside the Meander River. Camp kitchen. Pool.
MR: Map 3 B8

FURTHER INFORMATION

Deloraine Apex Caravan Park
Tel: 03 6362 2673
Camping fees: Unpowered from $25.00 per site/night for 2 people. Powered from $30.00 per site/night for 2 people.

THE RUGGED NORTH-WEST

WATER WISE

Fresh water for drinking and cooking is one aspect of camping which needs to be taken into consideration. You can't always rely on creeks and rivers – they may be polluted by animals, muddy or even dry. Allow around 7 litres of water per person per day – plus a couple of extra litres if you are heading into remote areas. We find storing water in a couple of 20 litre containers more convenient than in one larger container. Besides being easier to lift in and out of the vehicle and easier to handle around camp, if one container springs a leak you don't risk losing all your drinking water

66 Gowrie Park

The small village of Gowrie Park is located 14km south of Sheffield and accessed via the C136.

O'Neills Creek Reserve

Signposted access along the C136 road in Gowrie Park, 14km south of Sheffield. Suitable for big rigs. Bring drinking water and firewood.

GPS S:41 28.007 E:146 13.191

MR: Map 2 K8

FURTHER INFORMATION

Sheffield Visitor Information Centre

Tel: 03 6491 1179

Web: www.sheffieldcradleinfo.com.au

Camping fees: From $5.00 per site/night.

Maximum stay: 4 nights.

O'Neills Creek Reserve

67 Julius River Forest Reserve

Julius River Forest Reserve is located 46km south of Smithton. Access to the reserve is along the South Arthur Forest Drive which is signposted from the A2 highway at Smithton. Enjoy a walk through the cool temperate rainforest.

Julius River Forest camping area

Located 10km east of Kanunnah Bridge over Arthur River and 600m east of the Julius River Forest picnic area. Gravel road commences 1.8km east of Kanunnah Bridge. Six sites best suited for camper trailer, caravan, motorhome and campervan camping. Not suitable for tent based camping. Toilet facilities in picnic area.

GPS S:41 09.131 E:145 02.048

MR: Map 1 E6

FURTHER INFORMATION

Sustainable Timber Tasmania, Smithton

Tel: 03 6452 9100

THE RUGGED NORTH-WEST

68 Lake Barrington

This large lake is a popular venue for water-skiing, rowing, canoeing, fishing, boating and swimming. Located to the south of Devonport, access to the eastern shore is via West Kentish and to the western shore via Lower Wilmot. Camp only in the designated areas.

Kentish Park camping area

Located on the eastern shore of Lake Barrington, 6km west of West Kentish. Access is signposted off the C140 road south of Sheffield. Bring firewood.

GPS S:41 22.900 E:146 13.100

MR: Map 2 K7

Lake Barrington Park camping area

Located on the western shore of Lake Barrington, east of Wilmot and 8km south of Lower Wilmot. From Lower Wilmot travel south for 4.4km and take signposted Buxtons Road. Follow this road for 2.7km and turn into Lake Barrington Road, and after 600m track on right leads up hill to grassed camping area. Bring firewood.

GPS S:41 22.678 E:146 12.647

MR: Map 2 K7

FURTHER INFORMATION

Sheffield Visitor Information Centre

Tel: 03 6491 1179

Web: www.sheffieldcradleinfo.com.au

Maximum stay: 21 days in a 2 month period.

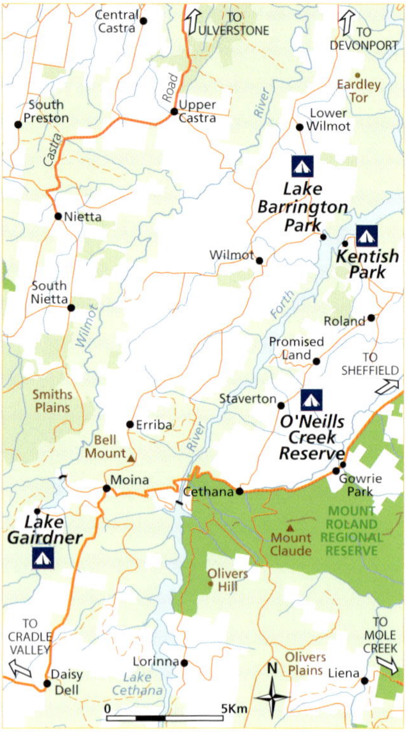

69 Lake Gairdner

Located to the west of Moina. Access is off the C132 road, 1km south of M

Lake Gairdner camping area

The access road (which is not signposted) is off the C132 road, 1km south of Moina. From the C132 travel for 4km to a small grassed area in the vicinity of bridge over Iris River. Open area with no shade. Bring drinking water and firewood.

GPS S:41 29.033 E:146 03.561
MR: Map 2 J8

FURTHER INFORMATION

Hydro Tasmania
Tel: 1300 360 441
Web: www.hydro.com.au
Maximum stay: 7 days.

70 Lake Mackintosh

Lake Mackintosh is adjacent to the town of Tullah. The lake is a hydro dam which offers anglers top-rate trout fishing.

Lake Mackintosh camping area

Located north of the dam wall via Mackintosh Dam Road, 6.3km north of Tullah. Dam road is signposted in Tullah. Site not accessible when dam water is flowing over spillway. Best suited for camper trailers, caravans, motorhomes and campervans, limited tent-based camping. No facilities, suitable for self-sufficient campers. Bring drinking water and firewood.

GPS S:41 41.129 E:145 39.396
MR: Map 6 H2

FURTHER INFORMATION

Hydro Tasmania
Tel: 1300 360 441
Web: www.hydro.com.au
West Coast Council
Tel: 03 6471 4700
Maximum stay: 7 days.

Lake Mackintosh camping area, Lake Mackintosh

71 Latrobe

Situated on the banks of the Mersey River, Latrobe's main street has 75 heritage-listed buildings. Other attractions of this historic town include the Australian Axemans Hall of Fame, scenic parklands, antiquities and crafts, fine foods and some excellent platypus viewing areas. Latrobe is located west of the Bass Highway with access signposted off the highway 20km south-east of Devonport.

Latrobe Motorhome Stop

R

Signposted access on Cotton Street in Latrobe. Designated area for fully self-contained motorhomes ie: units must have own fresh water storage, sealed grey water holding tank, sealed black water.
MR: Map 2 L6

FURTHER INFORMATION

Latrobe Visitor Information Centre
Tel: 03 6426 2240. Permit required from visitor information centre.
Web: www.latrobe.tas.gov.au
Maximum stay: 48 hours.

Suspension Bridge, Montezuma Falls, south of Rosebery

72 Marrawah

Marrawah is located 51km west of Smithton via the Bass Highway (A2). The coastline's rugged headlands receive the full force of the Roaring Forties from the Southern Ocean. Popular swimming, board riding and windsurfing area.

Green Point camping area

Located 2.4km west of Marrawah. Access via Beach Road off Green Point Road. Outdoor cold showers. Bring drinking water and firewood.

GPS S:40 54.566 E:144 40.738

MR: Map 1 C4

FURTHER INFORMATION

Circular Head Council
Tel: 03 6452 4800
Web: www.circularhead.tas.gov.au or www.stanley.com.au

Green Point camping area

73 Montagu Recreation Reserve

Montagu is located 15km west of Smithton along the C215 road. This coastal location is popular for water activities. Rips can be common, check with caretakers for safe swimming, fishing, canoeing and water-skiing sites.

Montagu Camping Ground

Located 4km north of Montagu. Accessed along Old Port Road, which is signposted off the C215 road 1km east of Montagu locality. Bring drinking water and firewood.

GPS S:40 44.735 E:144 58.643
MR: Map 1 D3

FURTHER INFORMATION

Caretaker

Tel: 0428 524 843. Bookings recommended for Christmas, long weekends and Easter. Camping area open from 1 November to 30 April. Opening dates may vary from year to year.

Circular Head Council

Tel: 03 6452 4800
Web: www.circularhead.tas.gov.au
Camping fees: Current fees available from caretaker during camping season.

Montagu Camping Ground

74 Peggs Beach Conservation Area

Located on the north coast between Stanley and Wynyard. Activities include fishing, swimming and beachcombing.

Black River camping area

Signposted access along the A2 (Bass Highway), 8.8km east of the Stanley turn-off (B21) and 2.2km west of Peggs Beach turn-off. Drive in 700m to start of camping areas. Suitable for big rigs. Very large area with some open and some shaded sites. Natural boat launch into river. **NB:** No fires on the ground, carry own firepot or brazier. Limited tank water, bring own drinking water and firewood.

GPS S:40 50.721 E:145 19.199

MR: Map 1 F4

Peggs Beach camping area

Signposted access along the A2 (Bass Highway), 2.2km east of Black River turn-off and 42km west of Wynyard. Camping area close to road. Limited sites for travellers as the camping area has permanent holiday sites. Beach boat launch nearby. Tank water, boil first or bring own drinking water. Bring firewood.

GPS S:40 51.199 E:145 21.030

MR: Map 1 F4

FURTHER INFORMATION

Parks & Wildlife Service Smithton

Tel: 03 6458 1480

Parks Pass: Not required.

Camping fees: From $13.00 per site/night up to 2 people.

Black River camping area

75 Penguin Area

Penguin is home to the large under cover Penguin Market which is held every Sunday showcasing a wonderful array of arts and crafts along with fresh produce. Situated between Devonport and Burnie, access to Penguin is signposted along the Bass Highway.

Halls Park

Signposted access along the Bass Highway at Sulphur Creek, 8km west of Penguin. Designated area for fully self-contained caravans, motorhomes and campervans ie: units must have own fresh water storage, sealed grey water holding tank, sealed black water.

MR: Map 2 J5

Preservation Bay Rest Area

Small area located at the Penguin Surf Club. From the Bass Highway take Preservation Drive and follow for 3.5km to the surf club car park. Rest area is the east of the surf club. Designated area for fully self-contained caravans, motorhomes and campervans ie: units must have own fresh water storage, sealed grey water holding tank, sealed black water.

MR: Map 2 J5

FURTHER INFORMATION

Penguin Visitor Information Centre
Tel: 03 6437 1421
Maximum stay: 48 hours.

76 Pieman River State Reserve

Corinna has a rich history, magnificent wilderness, bushwalks and good trout fishing. Take time out to enjoy a river cruise along the Pieman. Access to Corinna from the north is via the C247 road from Savage River (26km) or the C249 road (80km) which is 58km south of Smithton. From the south access is via the C249 road from Zeehan (48km), ferry crossing is required. Caravans note: maximum length (combination wheel base) for ferry is 9 metres.

Corinna Campground

Located in Corinna. Access via Savage River or Smithton from the north and via Zeehan from the south. Limited water, bring drinking water. Firewood supplied. No power.

GPS S:41 39.031 E:145 04.717
MR: Map 5 E1

FURTHER INFORMATION

Corinna Wilderness Experience
Tel: 03 6446 1170. Limited campsites. Bookings essential from November to May.
Web: www.corinna.com.au
Camping fees: From $40.00 per site/ night for 2 people. Cabin accommodation available.

Corinna Campground, Pieman River State Reserve

77 Port Sorell

Located 15km east of Devonport on the Rubicon River estuary. Close to Bass Strait beaches and popular water activities area.

Port Sorell Lions Club Caravan Park

Located on Meredith Street in Port Sorell on the eastern banks of Rubicon River. Fire pots and firewood available. Laundry facilities and childrens playground.

MR: Map 3 A6

FURTHER INFORMATION

Port Sorell Lions Club Caravan Park

Tel: 03 6428 7267 Bookings essential for peak periods, November to April.

Web: www.portsorellcaravanpark.com.au

Camping fees: Unpowered from $22.00 per site/night for 2 people. Powered from $33.00 per site/night for 2 people.

78 Railton

The town of Railton is located 13km south of Latrobe and 12km north-east of Sheffield. Walk the streets of Railton and enjoy the imaginative topiary display of over 100 figures in this unique outdoor gallery.

Railway Park

Access is along the Esplande in Railton. Designated area for fully self-contained caravans and motorhomes ie: units must have own fresh water storage, sealed grey water holding tank, sealed black water.
MR: Map 2 L7

FURTHER INFORMATION

Sheffield Visitor Information Centre
Tel: 03 6491 1179
Web: www.sheffieldcradleinfo.com.au
Maximum stay: 4 nights.

79 Riana

Riana is a small village in a dairy and produce region south of Penguin. Access via the B17 road from Penguin. Visit the nearby deer farm.

Riana Pioneer Park camping ground

Signposted access on Pine Road (B17) in Riana, 17km south of Penguin. Drinking water, bore water. Some firewood supplied.
GPS S:41 12.933 E:145 50.933
MR: Map 2 J6

FURTHER INFORMATION

Riana Pioneer Park Secretary/ Caretaker
Tel: 03 6111 4779 or 03 6437 6137
Web: www.pioneerpark.org.au
Camping fees: Unpowered from $12.00 per site/night for 2 people. Powered from $20.00 per site/night for 2 people. Fees collected daily.

The Nut, Stanley

80 Sheffield

Sheffield is known as 'The Town of Murals' and is situated 33km south of Devonport. There is a self-guided audio tour of the town's 50 beautiful murals depicting the life of a small Tasmanian rural town. As the gateway to Cradle Mountain, Sheffield is a wonderful base from which to explore and enjoy the region.

Sheffield Recreation Ground

Access is along Spring Street in Sheffield. Designated area for fully self-contained caravans and motorhomes ie: units must have own fresh water storage, sealed grey water holding tank, sealed black water.

MR: Map 2 K7

FURTHER INFORMATION

Sheffield Visitor Information Centre

Tel: 03 6491 1179
Web: www.sheffieldcradleinfo.com.au
Camping fees: From $5.00 per site/night.
Maximum stay: 4 nights.

Sheffield

THE RUGGED NORTH-WEST

81 Waratah

Located 67km south of Burnie via the Hampshire-Guildford Road. Waratah was once home to the world's richest tin mine and is only five minutes drive west of the Murchison Highway. The area has many activities for the visitor including gold panning, trout fishing and river cruises.

Waratah camping ground

Located on Smith Street in Waratah, behind council offices. Key access to toilet and shower facilities.

GPS S:41 26.733 E:145 31.967

MR: Map 1 G8

FURTHER INFORMATION

Waratah-Wynyard Shire Council, Waratah

Tel: 03 6439 7100. Hours: Mon to Fri 9am-5pm

Web: www.warwyn.tas.gov.au

Waratah Roadhouse

Tel: 03 6439 1110

Camping fees: Unpowered site from $22.00 per site/night. Powered site from $28.00 per site/night. A refundable key bond is required. Key available from council offices during business hours or from roadhouse after hours.

82 Wynyard

A former mining town, Wynyard is now a major service centre for the state's north-west. Located 12km west of Burnie, Wynyard is situated on the coast at the mouth of the Inglis River. Visit Fossil Bluff, Table Cape Lookout, enjoy a scenic walk along the Inglis River or try your luck fishing for trout in the Inglis and Flowerdale rivers.

Wynyard Showgrounds

Access on Jackson Street in Wynyard. Designated area for fully self-contained motorhomes ie: units must have own fresh water storage, sealed grey water holding tank, sealed black water.

MR: Map 2 H5

FURTHER INFORMATION

Wynyard Visitor Information Centre

Tel: 03 6443 8330

Web: www.visitwaratahwynyard.com.au

Maximum stay: 24 hours.

The Central Highland Lakes

THE CENTRAL HIGHLAND LAKES region offers some of the state's most magnificent mountain country. Visitors to the region have the opportunity to enjoy a stroll along one of a number of walking trails ranging from easy day walks – many are in the vicinity of Dove Lake at Cradle Mountain and Lake St Clair – to longer multi-day hikes such as the internationally famous Overland Track. In the centre of the region are the alpine wilderness areas of Walls of Jerusalem National Park and to the west is the world-renowned Cradle Mountain – Lake St Clair National Park, both offering excellent walking routes through breathtaking alpine scenery.

Further to the east, the numerous man-made lakes of the Central Plateau offer excellent fishing and boating opportunities. Those lucky enough may enjoy a catch of trout from one of the renown trout fisheries such as Great Lake, while those looking for seclusion can seek out remote camping sites on the banks of Woods Lake or Lagoon of Islands.

In the north of the region are Marakoopa and King Solomons Caves, both located within Mole Creek Karst National Park, while the interestingly named Devils Gullet is on the Great Western Tier.

Visitors should remember that weather conditions in the central highlands can change drastically, and must be prepared for all weather conditions, including snow, at any time of the year. It is not uncommon to have four seasons in a number of hours in some locations throughout this region. Late spring, summer and autumn are the preferred times to visit this diverse area.

BEST CAMPSITES!

- **Lake St Clair – Lake St Clair Tourist Park**
  Cradle Mountain – Lake St Clair National Park
- **Lower Liffey Reserve campsite**
  Liffey Falls State Reserve
- **Waterfall Valley Hut campsite**
  Cradle Mountain – Lake St Clair National Park
- **Lake Parangana bush camping**
  Lake Parangana
- **Pumphouse Bay Camping Ground**
  Arthurs Lake

83 Arthurs Lake

Located within the Central Plateau Protected Area, Arthurs Lake is a haven for the keen fisherfolk. Access to Arthurs Lake is along the Poatina Road (B51), south of Poatina and north of the A5 highway.

Pumphouse Bay Camping Ground

Signposted access along the Poatina Road (B51), 6km north of the A5 junction and 36km south of Poatina. Then drive in 800m to camping area. Woodfired hot showers, generally October to April. Boil drinking water first. Gather own firewood.

GPS S:41 59.116 E:146 51.640
MR: Map 7 C3

Pumphouse Bay Camping Ground

Jonah Bay Camping Ground

Signposted access along the Poatina Road (B51), 4.2km north of the Pumphouse Bay access road and 32km south of Poatina. Then drive in 3.1km to road junction, turn right and follow for 1.7km to camping area. Grassed, shaded sites beside the lake. Bring drinking water and firewood.

GPS S:41 57.522 E:146 54.150
MR: Map 7 C3

Jonah Bay Camping Ground

FURTHER INFORMATION

Central Highlands Council
Tel: 03 6259 5503
Web: www.centralhighlands.tas.gov.au
Camping fees: From $4.00 per adult/night and $2.00 per child/night. Fees payable at self-registration stations.

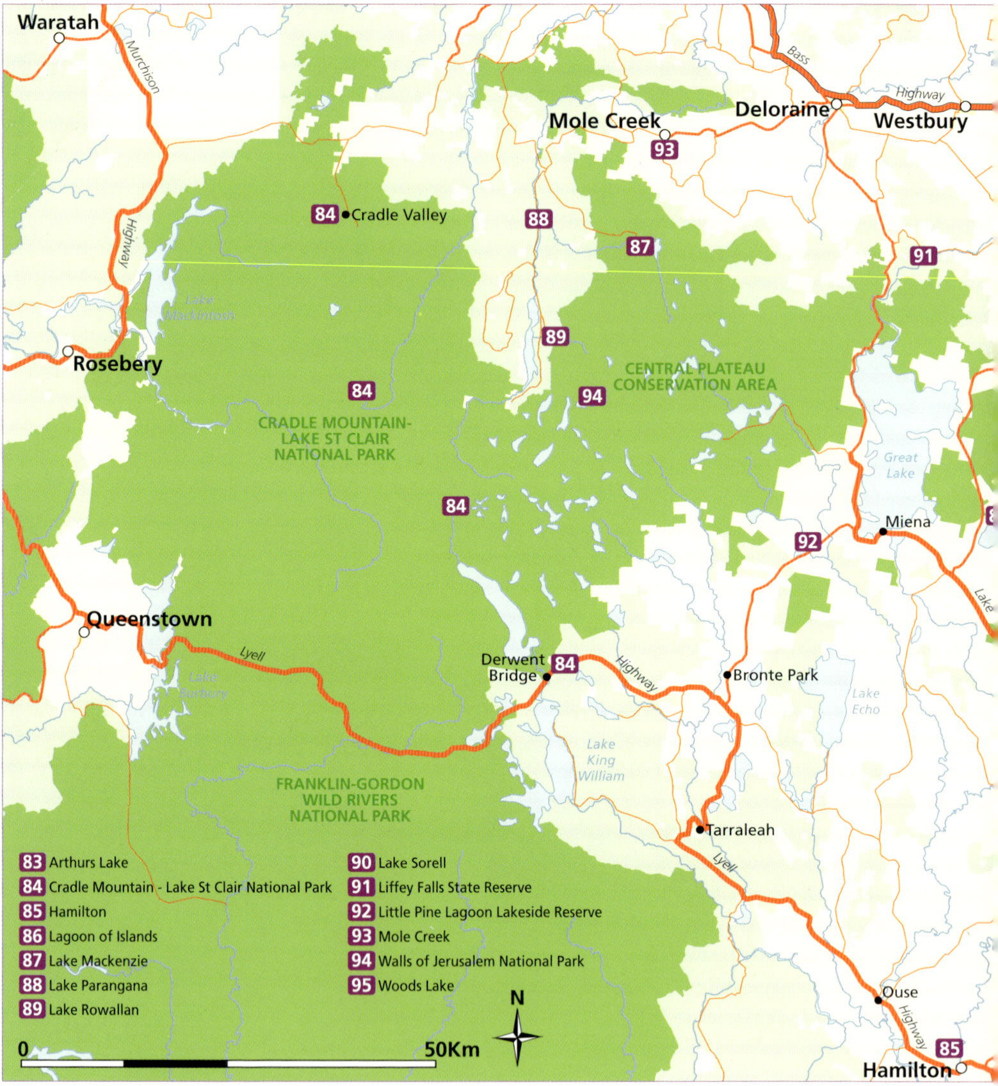

CRADLE MOUNTAIN DAY WALKS

There are four popular day walks that can be undertaken by visitors to Cradle Mountain. Of these, easily the most popular is the 2 hour (6km) Dove Lake Circuit—this easy grade walk will take you right around Dove Lake with superb vistas of Cradle Mountain. Those after a short stroll (20 minutes) may wish to amble along the Enchanted Walk which starts at the visitor centre and meanders through old growth rainforest.

The Crater Lake Circuit Walk is a 2 hour walk and a good option for cold, wet and windy days as it is more protected. Serious day walkers can tackle the Cradle Mountain Summit Walk, an 8 hour return climb to the imposing peak of Cradle Mountain via Lake Lilla and Marions Lookout.

Details of these walks plus a host of others around the state can be found in the Tasmania's 60 Great Short Walks brochure.

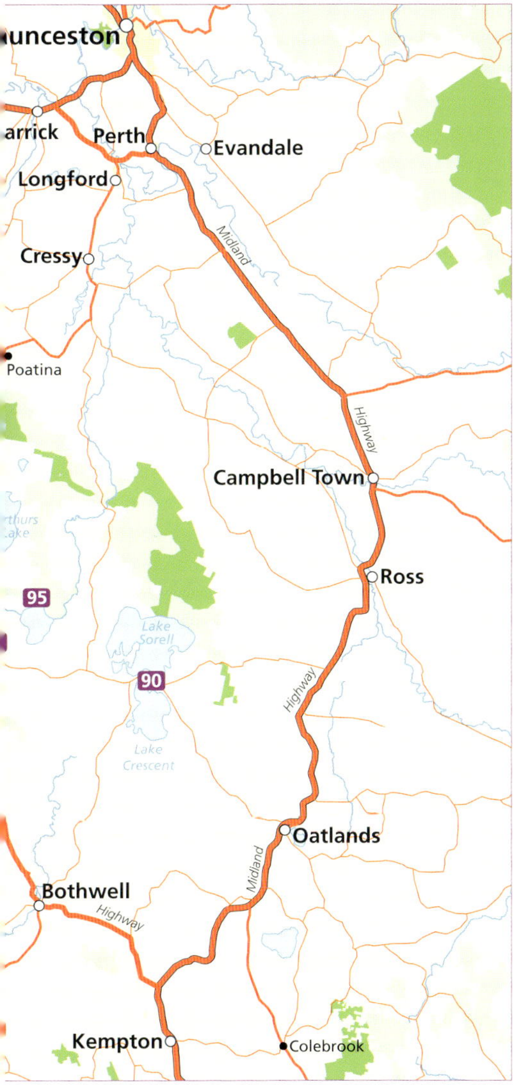

RECREATIONAL
FISHING LICENCES

If you intend dangling a line in the hope of hooking a tasty trout in Tasmania's inland waterways then you are required to obtain a Recreational Fishing Licence. These are available in selected centres or by contacting the Inland Fisheries Service on 03 6165 3808 or at www.ifs.tas.gov.au for details.

THE CENTRAL HIGHLAND LAKES

Cradle Mountain

84 Cradle Mountain - Lake St Clair National Park

Cradle Mountain – Lake St Clair National Park is one of Tasmania's most popular parks with many visitors coming to walk the world-renowned Overland Track. The park features the rugged contours of Cradle Mountain and its surrounding alpine environs as its northern centerpiece while to the south is Lake St Clair, the deepest lake in Australia, with its beautiful forests. This large national park is part of the Tasmanian Wilderness World Heritage Area. Numerous day walks of varying lengths are also on offer.

Cradle Mountain – Discovery Holiday Park Cradle Mountain

Signposted access along Cradle Mountain Road, 54km south-west of Sheffield and 2km before park's entry station. Suitable for big rigs. Camp kitchen and laundry facilities.

GPS S:41 34.788 E:145 56.198

MR: Map 6 I1

FURTHER INFORMATION

Discovery Holiday Park Cradle Mountain

Tel: 03 6492 1395 or 1800 068 574. Bookings for powered sites recommended during peak period, November to May.

Web: www.discoveryholidayparks.com.au

Parks Pass: Not required.

Camping fees: Contact office for current fee structure. This park offers off-peak, peak and shoulder periods. Cabin and backpacker accommodation available.

Lake St Clair – Lake St Clair Tourist Park

Signposted access along Lake St Clair Road, 5km north-west of the Lyell Highway (A10) at Derwent Bridge. Token-operated showers, tokens from office. Laundry facilities. Firewood supplied.

GPS S:42 06.925 E:146 10.630

MR: Map 6 K4

FURTHER INFORMATION

Lake St Clair Lodge and Tourist Park

Tel: 03 6289 1137. Bookings for powered sites recommended during January.

Web: www.lakestclairlodge.com.au

Parks Pass: Required.

Camping fees: Contact office for current fee structure. This park offers off-peak, peak and shoulder periods. Cabin and backpacker accommodation available.

Lake St Clair - Lake St Clair Tourist Park

The Overland Track camping areas

Six-day walking track from Cradle Valley to Lake St Clair. Self-sufficient experienced walkers. Gas/fuel stove only. Rainwater tanks at huts. Remember: Pack it in/Pack it out.

Cradle Valley **MR:** Map 6 I1

Waterfall Valley Hut: 10km from Waldheim (6 hours)

GPS S:41 421.884 E:145 56.812

Windermere Hut: 7.5km from Waterfall Valley Hut (3 hours)

GPS S:41 46.295 E:145 57.376

New Pelion Hut: 16.5km from Windermere Hut (6 hours)

GPS S:41 49.772 E:146 02.781

Kia Ora Hut: 10km from New Pelion Hut (3 hours)

GPS S:41 53.531 E:146 04.890

Bert Nichols (Windy Ridge) Hut: 10km from Kia Ora Hut (4 hours)

GPS S:41 56.024 E:146 05.256

Narcissus Hut: 9km from Bert Nichols Hut (3 hours)

GPS S:42 00.752 E:146 06.097

Lake St Clair **MR:** Map 6 K4

Side trip camping areas:

Scott Kilvert Memorial Hut at Lake Rodway

Pine Valley Hut at Pine Valley

Echo Point Hut at Echo Point

FURTHER INFORMATION

Parks & Wildlife Service Visitor Centres

Cradle Mountain **tel:** 03 6492 1110

Lake St Clair **tel:** 03 6289 1172

A booking system and fee applies to walk the Overland Track from 1 November to 30 April. Outside of this period bookings and fees do not apply. Bookings can be made over the phone contact The Overland Track Administrator on **tel:** 03 6165 4254, or online by visiting website: www.overlandtrack.com.au, or in person at the above visitor information centres.

Parks Pass: Required.

Overland Track Fees: From $200.00 per adult and $160.00 per child (5 to 17 years)/ seniors/pension consessionaires.

NB: All walkers must register and deregister at trackheads, it is also recommended to have a nominated contact person. Carry large scale maps. There are a number of specialised walking publications for the Overland Track.

Cradle Mountain day walk

85 Hamilton

The historic village of Hamilton is located on the A10 highway 75km north-west of Hobart beside the Clyde River. There are numerous historic buildings dating as far back as the 1830s, many of which were built of local sandstone by convict labor.

Hamilton Camping Ground

Signposted access along River Street (Tarleton Street) in Hamilton at the western end of town. Coin-operated showers. Grassed areas. Laundry facilities, key access.

GPS S:42 33.550 E:146 49.833
MR: Map 7 C7

FURTHER INFORMATION

Central Highlands Council
Tel: 03 6286 3202. Key access to laundry, refundable key deposit applies. Key available from council offices located on Tarleton Street.
Web: www.centralhighlands.tas.gov.au
Camping fees: From $5.00 per site/night.
Maximum stay: 3 nights.

86 Lagoon of Islands

Situated in the Central Plateau region, access to the Lagoon of Islands is via the Interlaken Road off the A5 Highway. Popular fishing spot.

Camping is no longer possible

Waterfall Valley campsite, Overland Walking Track

87 Lake Mackenzie

Access via Lake Mackenzie Road off the C171 road, which leaves the C138 road, 20km west of Mole Creek. Travel for 22km to this open campsite and fishing area.

Lake Mackenzie bush camping

Located 22km along Lake Mackenzie Road at the dam. Lake Mackenzie Road is signposted off the C171 road 300m south of its junction with the C138. Access road may be closed during bad weather. Limited tent-based camping due to rocky ground. Suitable for off-road camper trailers. Small exposed site best suited to anglers. Gas/fuel stove preferred. Bring drinking water and firewood.

GPS S:41 40.594 E:146 22.763

MR: Map 6 L1

FURTHER INFORMATION

Hydro Tasmania

Tel: 1300 360 441

Web: www.hydro.com.au

Maximum stay: 7 days.

88 Lake Parangana

Lake Parangana is located to the west of Mole Creek and accessed off the C171, which is signposted 20km west of Mole Creek. The lake's access track is through the picnic area which is 7.4km south of the C171 and C138 junction, and 1.2km south of the dam wall.

Lake Parangana bush camping

Access road is 1.2km south of the Parangana Dam wall through the picnic area, 7.4km along the C171 road. Dispersed bush camping on western foreshore of lake. Some open sites and some good protected sites back from the water among vegetation. Gas/fuel stove preferred. Bring drinking water, or boil from lake.

GPS S:41 38.642 E:146 13.515

MR: Map 6 K1

FURTHER INFORMATION

Hydro Tasmania

Tel: 1300 360 441

Web: www.hydro.com.au

Maximum stay: 7 days.

89 Lake Rowallan

Lake Rowallan is situated south of Lake Parangana and is accessed off the C171, which is signposted 20km west of Mole Creek. The lake's dam wall is 9.7km south of the Lake Parangana access track. Bush camping on the lake's eastern foreshore south of the dam and bush campsites beside the river north of the dam.

Lake Rowallan bush camping

Located south of Lake Parangana and accessed along the C171. Numerous access tracks lead off the C171 to bush camping areas on the lake's eastern foreshore south of the dam wall, and beside the river north of the dam wall. Boat ramps are signposted on the south side of the dam wall. Bring drinking water, or boil water from lake or river. Bring firewood. Gas/fuel stove preferred.

GPS S:41 44.142 E:146 13.176

MR: Map 6 K2

FURTHER INFORMATION

Hydro Tasmania

Tel: 1300 360 441

Web: www.hydro.com.au

Maximum stay: 7 days.

90 Lake Sorell

Lake Sorell is within the Central Plateau Conservation/Protected area. Access from the east is via the gravel Interlaken road (C526) off the A1 highway (this road has some steep sections and is not recommended for caravans), 12km south of Ross or the Interlaken road (C527) from Oatlands. Access is also possible via the C527 road from Bothwelll to the south and from the west via the C528 off the A5 highway.

Dago Point camping area

GPS S:42 07.887 E:147 09.914
MR: Map 7 D4

Signposted access along the Interlaken Road at Interlaken, 26.4km west of the A1 via the C526 and 26km east of the A5 via the C527. Turn-off is 2.5km west of the C528 (Bothwell) road. Then drive in 300m to playground, turn left for 200m to reach large camping area with shaded and grassed individual sites. Bring firewood.

FURTHER INFORMATION

Parks & Wildlife Service Great Western Tiers
Tel: 03 6701 2104
Parks Pass: Not required.
NB: Fishing is prohibited.

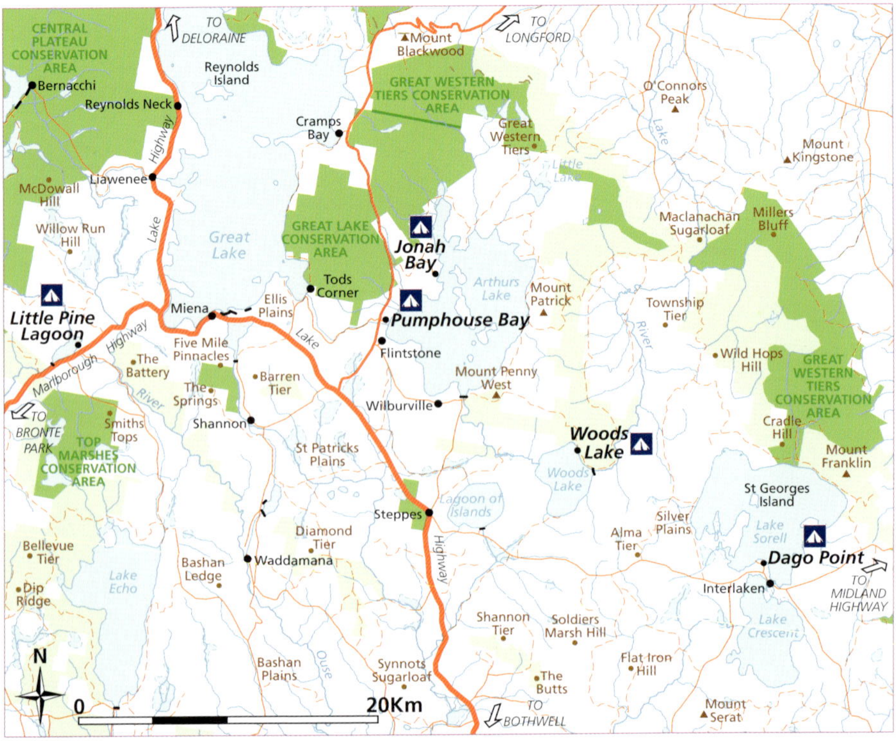

91 Liffey Falls State Reserve

This scenic reserve is nestled on the slopes of the Great Western Tiers amongst rainforest. Along with Liffey Falls there are a number of smaller falls within the reserve. Enjoy the nature walk through tree ferns and tall eucalypts. The reserve is 15km west of Bracknell and 7km west of the locality of Liffey. Accessed along the C513, from the west off the A5 and from the east via Gulf Road/Liffey Road (C513).

Lower Liffey Reserve campsite

Camping area located at the lower carpark of Liffey Falls. Access is signposted off the C513 road, 7km west of the locality of Liffey – this is the recommended access for caravans, trailers and motorhomes. Alternative access can be made from the west off the A5 (this access road has steep and narrow sections). Access from the A5 highway is signposted 23km south of Deloraine. From the highway travel for 1.9km to a Y-junction. The road on the right at junction leads to the falls top carpark and walking track (this road is not suitable for trailers, caravans or motorhomes). At junction keep left and follow the signposting to Liffey for a further 5.8km to the signposted Liffey Falls/Lower Track road. Then drive in 700m to the nicely shaded and grassed camping area. Bring drinking water and firewood.

GPS S:41 40.994 E:146 46.932
MR: Map 7 B1

FURTHER INFORMATION

Parks & Wildlife Service Prospect
Tel: 03 6777 2179
Parks Pass: Not required.

Lower Liffey Reserve campsite

92 Little Pine Lagoon Lakeside Reserve

Located south-west of Miena, Little Pine Lagoon Lakeside Reserve is accessed along the B11 road, 7.4km south of its junction with the A5 highway. The B11 road is signposted off the A5 2.6km west of Miena and 67km south of Deloraine. The reserve is located close to the road and offers fishing and boating opportunities.

Little Pine Lagoon Lakeside Reserve camping area

Signposted access along the B11 road, 7.4km south of the A5 highway. Then drive in 500m from B11 to self-registration station and camping areas. One area for camper trailers and caravans, and one area for tent-based camping. Bring drinking water. Gas/fuel stove only.

GPS S:41 59.977 E:146 36.696

MR: Map 7 A4

FURTHER INFORMATION

Parks & Wildlife Service Great Western Tiers

Tel: 03 6701 2104

Parks Pass: Not required.

Camping fees: From $3.00 per adult/night. Fees payable at self-registration station.

Little Pine Lagoon camping area

93 Mole Creek

Mole Creek is an ideal location to base yourself whilst exploring the nearby lakes and King Solomons and Marakoopa caves. Mole Creek is on the B12 road 23km west of Deloraine.

Mole Creek Caravan Park

Signposted access at junction of B12 and C137 roads, 3.2km west of Mole Creek village. Situated beside creek. Coin-operated showers. Camp kitchen and laundry facilities. Fires only allowed on the creek side of the camping area. Firewood supplied.

GPS S:41 33.101 E:146 21.629

MR: Map 6 L1

FURTHER INFORMATION

Mole Creek Caravan Park

Tel: 03 6363 1150

Web: www.molecreek.net.au

Camping fees: Unpowered from $20.00 per site/night for 2 people. Powered from $25.00 per site/night for 2 people. Fees payable to caretaker. On-site accommodation available.

Mole Creek Caravan Park

Woods Lake

94 Walls of Jerusalem National Park

The park features majestic mountain scenery and alpine lakes. There is no vehicle access within the park—day or overnight walkers only. The park is 23km from the C171 junction via the Walls of Jerusalem Track off the Mersey Forest Road (C171). The C171 is 20km west of Mole Creek. Walkers must be aware and ready for dramatic weather changes whilst visiting this park.

Wild Dog Creek walk-in camping area

Located 2 to 3 hours walk from car park. Access to car park is signposted along the C171 road. Walk-in bush campsites for self-sufficient walkers. Some tank water. Gas/fuel stove only.

MR: Map 6 K2

FURTHER INFORMATION

Parks & Wildlife Service Great Western Tiers

Tel: 03 6701 2104

Parks Pass: Required.

Walkers must register and deregister at registration station along track near car park and carry large scale maps. Contact ranger for further details and information.

94 Woods Lake

Woods Lake is a popular fishing and boating destination, with remote bush camping around the lake's foreshore. Access to Woods Lake is signposted off Arthurs Lake Road (C525), which is signposted off the B51 highway 4.5km north of the B51 and A5 highway junction, and 38km south of Poatina. The lake's foreshore is located 12km south-east of its turn off from Arthurs Lake Road. Unsealed access road can be rough. AWD or 4WD vehicle recommended, especially if towing.

Woods Lake bush camping

From the B51 highway take the signposted Arthurs Lake Road (C525) for 8.6km to the signposted Woods Lake access track. Then travel for 1.2km to a Y-junction and keep right along the signposted Woods Lake road. Travel for 11km to Woods Lake boat ramp and to numerous tracks which lead to bush campsites along the lake's foreshore. No facilities, suitable for self-sufficient campers. Bring drinking water and firewood.

GPS S:42 03.878 E:147 00.902

MR: Map 7 C4

FURTHER INFORMATION

Hydro Tasmania

Tel: 1300 360 441

Web: www.hydro.com.au

Maximum stay: 7 days.

Roadside Rest Areas

REST AREA/TOWN	LOCATION	TOILET	TABLE	FIREPLACE	SHELTER	WATER	MAP
NORTH-EAST REGION							
Blue Tier Picnic Area	Lottah Road, 4k N of Lottah	✓	✓	✓	✓		4 I6
Conaro Rest Area	Midland Highway 10km N of Campbell Town	✓	✓	✓	✓	✓	7 F2
Derby Park Picnic Area	On A3 at western end of town	✓	✓	✓	✓		4 G6
Evercreech Forest Reserve Picnic Area	13.4km NE of Mathinna on Egans Road via Clayton Road	✓	✓	✓	✓		4 H7
Halls Falls Picnic Area	On Anchor Road, 900m N of the A3		✓				4 I6
Hardings Falls Forest Reserve Picnic Area	Turn off is 36.1km N of the B34 road via the MS and MG roads, and 25.5km N of Meetus Falls	✓	✓				8 I3
Hollybank Forest Picnic Area	20km NE of Launceston via the B81	✓		✓	✓		3 D7
Lookout/Picnic Area	On A3 highway 14km N of Targa and 16km S of Scottsdale	✓	✓	✓	✓		3 E6
Maa Mon Chin Picnic Area	3.5km W of Weldborough Hotel via Mount Paris Dam Road						4 H6
Mathinna Falls Picnic Area	10.1km N of Mathinna on Waterfall Gully Road, via Clayton Road	✓	✓				4 H7
Minnie Jessop Picnic Ground	2.2km west of Maa Mon Chin Picnic Area via Mount Paris Dam Road		✓				4 H6
Parramatta Creek Rest Area	Bass Highway S of Sassafras	✓	✓	✓	✓	✓	2 L6
Ralphs Falls Picnic Area	18.6km W of Pyengana via Ringarooma Road	✓	✓	✓	✓	✓	4 H6
Springfield Picnic Area	13.3km south of Scottsdale via the C406 South Springfield Road		✓	✓			3 F6
SOUTH-EAST REGION							
Cradoc Park Picnic Area	Cradoc on the B68 highway, south of Huonville	✓	✓		✓		11 D3
Denison Canal Park	On A9 highway at Dunalley	✓	✓		✓		12 G2
Gordon Jetty Picnic Area	On B68 road at Gordon	✓	✓	✓			11 E4
Mavista Picnic Area, Bruny Island	On Resolution Road, which is 2.1km S of Adventure Bay via Lockleys Road	✓	✓				11 E5
Meetus Falls Picnic Area	On MS Road, which is 10.6km N of the B34 road		✓	✓	✓		8 H3
Sandspit Picnic Area	On Wielangta Road Forest Drive, 15km N of the A9		✓	✓	✓		12 H1
Spring Beach Picnic Area	Access off the C320 road, 4.2km S of Orford	✓	✓	✓	✓		8 H7
St Peters Pass Rest Area	Midland Highway, 3km S of Woodbury and 10km N of Oatlands	✓	✓	✓	✓	✓	7 E5
Three Thumbs Picnic Area	Access off Wielangta Forest Drive, 5km S of the A3 at Orford		✓		✓	✓	8 H8

REST AREAS

SOUTH-WEST REGION

REST AREA/TOWN	LOCATION	TOILET	TABLE	FIREPLACE	SHELTER	WATER	MAP
Calvert Park Picnic Area	Beside Huon River at Judbury, 13km W of Huonville via Glen Huon Road	✓	✓	✓	✓		11 C3
Ellendale Picnic Area	Located at fire station in village of Ellendale on C608 road	✓	✓	✓	✓		7 B8
Glen Huon Memorial Park	8.9k mW of Huonville via Glen Huon Road		✓		✓		11 C3
Grace Nicholas Park	At northern end of bridge in village of Ouse on A10 highway		✓		✓	✓	7 B7
Henty Dunes Picnic Area	Signposted access of B27 highway, 13km N of Strahan		✓		✓		5 F4
Nive River Picnic Area	On A10 highway at power station, 3.3km N of the northern access road to Tarraleah	✓	✓	✓	✓	✓	6 L6
Swan Basin Picnic Area	9.4km S of Strahan along C251 road		✓	✓			5 F5

A1 – QUEENSTOWN TO DERWENT BRIDGE

REST AREA/TOWN	LOCATION	TOILET	TABLE	FIREPLACE	SHELTER	WATER	MAP
Nelson Falls Walking Track	27km E of Queenstown	✓					6 H4
Donaghy Hill Lookout & Walk	51km E of Queenstown						6 I5

B61 ROAD – MAYDENA TO STRATHGORDON

REST AREA/TOWN	LOCATION	TOILET	TABLE	FIREPLACE	SHELTER	WATER	MAP
Styx Valley Big Tree Reserve	Turn off is 3km W of Maydena, then 15km S						11 A1
Needles Picnic Area	24km W of Maydena	✓	✓		✓		10 L1
Boyd Lookout	3.4km W of Scotts Peak Dam Road						10 K1
Mt Wedge Walking Track	12.6km W of Scotts Peak Dam Road						10 K2
Wedge River Picnic Area	17.8km W of Scotts Peak Dam Road	✓	✓	✓	✓	✓	10 K2

Blue Tier Picnic Area

REST AREA/TOWN	LOCATION	TOILET	TABLE	FIREPLACE	SHELTER	WATER	MAP
NORTH-WEST REGION							
Alma Reserve Picnic Area	Beside river on Wilmot Road, 12.4km S of Forth		✓	✓			2 K6
Dip Falls Picnic Area	On C225 road, 11.9km S of Mawbanna and 26.6km S of A2 highway	✓	✓	✓	✓		1 F5
Fossey River Rest Area	On A10 highway, 2km S of B23 junction	✓	✓	✓	✓		2 H8
Hellyer Gorge State Reserve Rest Area	On A10 highway, 39km S of A2	✓	✓		✓		2 H6
Leven Canyon Picnic Area	Access along C128 road, 9km SW of Nietta	✓	✓	✓		✓	2 J7
Oldina Picnic Area	Access via C235, 7km SW of Wynyard	✓	✓	✓	✓		2 H5
Peggs Beach Picnic Area	On A2 highway, 1.1km E of Peggs Beach CA	✓	✓	✓			1 F4
Sisters Beach Rest Area	At end of East Boulevard at Sisters Beach	✓	✓	✓	✓		2 G4
Stitt Park Picnic Area	South of Rosebery shopping village beside Stitt River	✓	✓	✓			6 G2
Warrawee Forest Reserve Picnic Area	Beside Mersey River, 6km S of Latrobe	✓	✓	✓			2 L6
SOUTH ARTHUR FOREST DRIVE							
Kanunnah Bridge Picnic Area	Beside Arthur River, 36.5km S of Smithton on B22 road		✓	✓	✓	✓	1 E6
Sumac Lookout	1.8km E of Kanunnah Bridge		✓				1 E6
Julius River Forest Reserve Picnic Area	7.6km E of Sumac Lookout	✓	✓	✓	✓		1 E6
Lake Chisholm Forest Reserve	Walk to lake. Turn off is 2.8km E of Julius River						1 E6
Dempster Lookout	Turn off is 2.8km E of Lake Chisholm turn off						1 E6
Rapid River Picnic Area	Located 4.1km N of Dempster Lookout turn off		✓				1 E6
Milkshakes Forest Reserve Picnic Area	Turn off is 13.7km N of Rapid River PA, then 6.5km to picnic area	✓	✓	✓	✓	✓	1 E5
Tayatea Bridge Picnic Area	Located 5.9km N of Milkshakes Forest Reserve PA access track, SE of Trowutta		✓	✓			1 E5

REST AREA/TOWN	LOCATION	TOILET	TABLE	FIREPLACE	SHELTER	WATER	MAP
WESTERN EXPLORER – ARTHUR RIVER TO CORINNA							
Gardiner Point Picnic Area	On Airey Street at Edge of the World. Turn off is south of the bridge over Arthur River.	✓	✓				1 C5
Lindsay River Crossing	Small clearing beside the road on south side of bridge, 52.8km S of Arthur River						1 D7
Donaldson River Crossing	Small clearing beside the road on north side of bridge, 82.6km S of Arthur River						1 E8
Longback Walk & Scenic Lookout	Signposted 96.4km S of Arthur River						5 E1
Scenic Lookout	Signposted 99.9km S of Arthur River						5 E1
Guthrie Creek Crossing	Small clearing beside the road on south side of bridge, 104.6km S of Arthur River						5 E1
Corinna Picnic Area	Beside Pieman River near ferry, 110.8km S of Arthur River	✓	✓	✓	✓		5 E1
CENTRAL HIGHLAND LAKES REGION							
Liffey Falls Picnic Area	Picnic area and walking tracks, 5.7km E of A5 highway via C153	✓	✓	✓	✓		7 B2
Meander Forest Reserve Picnic Area	Access via C167, south of Meander	✓	✓	✓	✓		7 A1
Mersey White Water Forest Reserve Picnic Area	Located 7km S of Lake Parangana	✓	✓	✓	✓		6 K1
Steppes Historic Site Picnic Area	Adjacent to historic site at Steppes on A5 highway, 34km N of Bothwell	✓					7 C4

Milkshakes Forest Reserve Picnic Area

Esperance camping site, Southern Forests

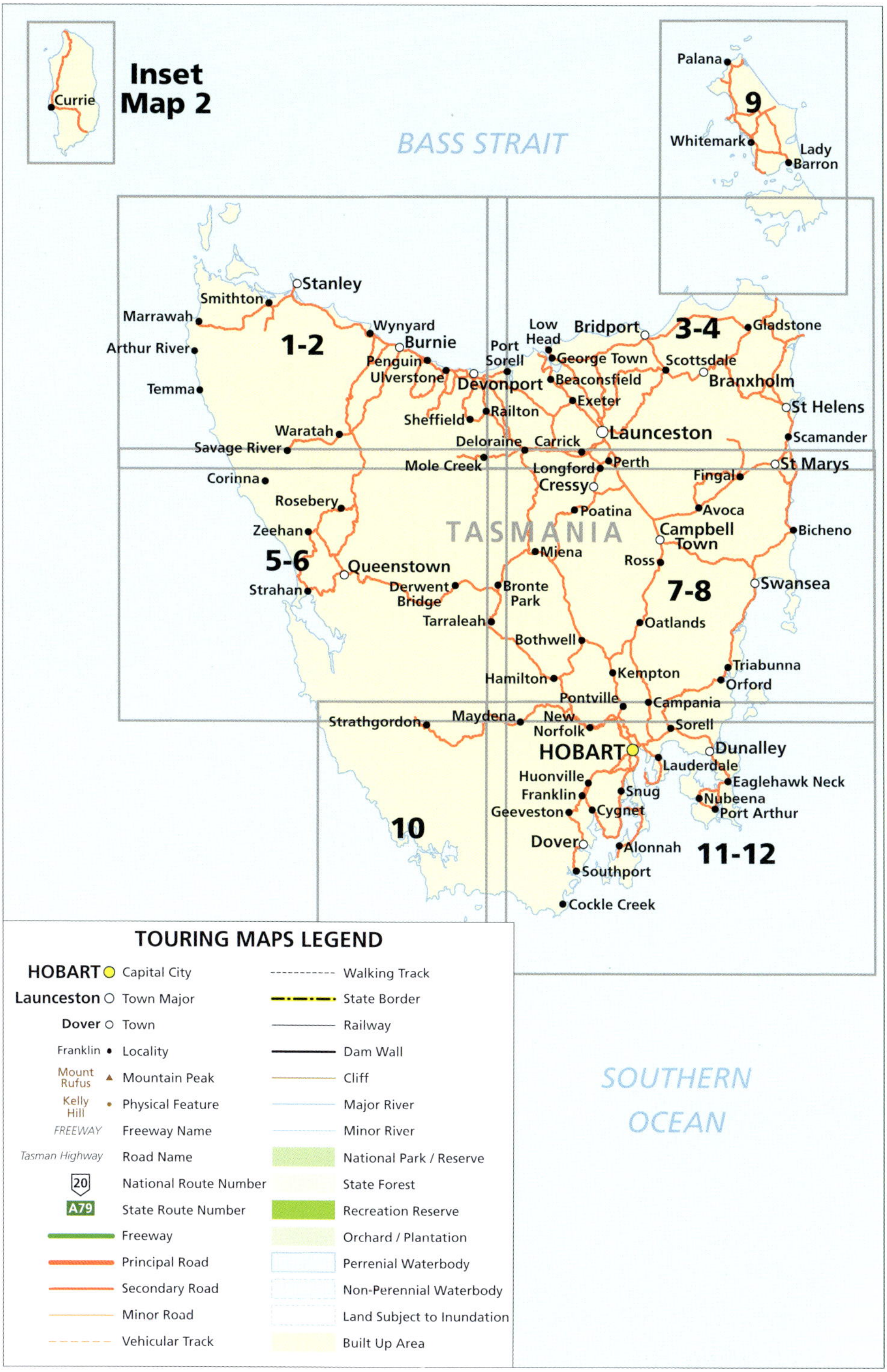
Inset Map 2
Currie
Palana
9
Whitemark
Lady Barron
BASS STRAIT
1-2
3-4
5-6
7-8
10
11-12
Stanley
Smithton
Marrawah
Arthur River
Temma
Wynyard
Burnie
Penguin
Ulverstone
Devonport
Port Sorell
Low Head
Bridport
Gladstone
George Town
Scottsdale
Branxholm
Beaconsfield
Exeter
St Helens
Sheffield
Railton
Launceston
Scamander
Waratah
Savage River
Deloraine
Carrick
Mole Creek
Perth
St Marys
Longford
Corinna
Cressy
Fingal
Rosebery
Poatina
Avoca
Zeehan
TASMANIA
Campbell Town
Bicheno
Miena
Ross
Queenstown
Strahan
Derwent Bridge
Bronte Park
Swansea
Tarraleah
Oatlands
Bothwell
Triabunna
Kempton
Hamilton
Orford
Pontville
Campania
Strathgordon
Maydena
New Norfolk
Sorell
HOBART
Dunalley
Lauderdale
Huonville
Eaglehawk Neck
Snug
Franklin
Nubeena
Geeveston
Cygnet
Port Arthur
Dover
Alonnah
Southport
Cockle Creek
SOUTHERN OCEAN
TOURING MAPS LEGEND
HOBART Capital City
Launceston Town Major
Dover Town
Franklin Locality
Mount Rufus Mountain Peak
Kelly Hill Physical Feature
FREEWAY Freeway Name
Tasman Highway Road Name
20 National Route Number
A79 State Route Number
Freeway
Principal Road
Secondary Road
Minor Road
Vehicular Track
Walking Track
State Border
Railway
Dam Wall
Cliff
Major River
Minor River
National Park / Reserve
State Forest
Recreation Reserve
Orchard / Plantation
Perrenial Waterbody
Non-Perennial Waterbody
Land Subject to Inundation
Built Up Area

A
B
C
D
E
F
1
2
3
4
5
6
7
8
Cape Keraudren
Cape Rochon
THREE HUMMOCK ISLAND STATE RESERVE
Cape Adamson
Cuvier Point
Hope Channel
HUNTER ISLAND CONSERVATION AREA
Cave Bay
Hunter Passage
Walker Channel
Woolnorth Point
Ransonnet Bay
Boullanger Bay
Robbins Island
Guyton Point
Cape Grim
Cape Elie
North Point
Flat Topped Bluff
Big Bay
Perkins Bay
Stanley
Bluff Point
West Montagu
Montagu
Dodgers Point
Scopus
Duck Bay
Tatlows Folly
Leesville
Jims Plain
Montagu Plains
Smithton
Wiltshire
Forest
Broadmeadows
Mount Cameron West
SOUTHERN OCEAN
Highway
South Forest
Mengha
Green Point
Hays Tier
Christmas Hills
Irishtown
Marrawah
Redpa
Togari
Brittons Swamp
Alcomie
Bass
Rainbow Hill
Eurebia
Mawbanna
West Point
A2
Lileah
ARTHUR-PIEMAN CONSERVATION AREA
Edith Creek
Seymour Hill
Nabageena
Mawson Bay
Roger River
Bluff Hill Point
Roger River West
Trowutta
Wedge Plains
Arthur River
Gardiner Point
River
Milkshake Hills
Arthur
Dunns Plain
Sundown Point
Luncheon Hill
Holder Plains
Nelson Bay
Forked Tree Hill
Couta Rocks
Frankland
Rapid
Lost Hill
DONALDSON RIVER NATURE RECREATION AREA
River
Temma
River
Hazard Bay
Balfour
Mount Balfour
Mount Frankland
Mount Bertha
Ordnance Point
ARTHUR-PIEMAN CONSERVATION AREA
Mount Hazelton
Kenneth Bay
Pyramid Hill
Mount Lily
Mount Holloway
River
Sandy Cape
Mount Bolton
Caudrys Hill
Mount Edith
Mount Norfolk
Norfolk Range
Savage
Mount Vero
Mount Sunday
Savage River
Mount Meredith
N
0
50km
Joins Map 5

G
H
I
J
K
L
Joins Map 3
1
2
3
4
5
6
7
8
BASS STRAIT
Cape Wickham
Cape Farewell
Wickham Hill
Phoques Bay
Egg Lagoon
Lavinia Point
Cooper Bluff
Whistler Point
Yambacoona
Counsel Hill
Reekara
King Island
Sea Elephant
Loorana
Sea Elephant Bay
Naracoopa
Currie
Parenna
Pegarah
Mary Hill
Yarra Creek
Lymwood
Gentle Annie
Bold Head
Fitzmaurice Bay
Grassy
Cataraqui Point
Pearshape
Mount Stanley
Seal Point
Surprise Bay
Seal Bay
Stokes Point
Rocky Cape Beach
Hellyer
Rocky Cape
Sisters Hills
Sisters Beach
Montumana
Boat Harbour
Table Cape
A2
Flowerdale
Wynyard
Myalla
Seabrook
Doctors Rocks
Lapoinya
Milabena
Dip Range
Camdale
Somerset
Burnie
Meunna Hills
Calder
Oldina
A10
Meunna
Preolenna
Elliott
Heybridge
Sulphur Creek
Mount Myrtle
Penguin
Pruarra Hill
Yolla
South Elliott
Stowport
Point Sorell
Campbell Range
Ridgley
Cuprona
West Pine
Turners Beach
Hawley Beach
Henrietta
Natone
Ferndene
1
Leith
Shearwater
Takone
Camena
Ulverstone
Devonport
West Takone
Gawler
Forth
Don
Wesley Vale
Taylors Hill
Tewkesbury
Highclere
Riana
Mount Riana
Moriarty
Mount Leslie
Upper Natone
North Motton
Abbotsham
Quoiba
Spreyton
Latrobe
Oonah
B18
South Riana
Mount Lorymer
Spalford
Kindred
Melrose
Paloona
Hellyer Gorge
Hampshire
Sprent
Bonneys Tier
Mount Housetop
Preston
Lower Barrington
Sassafras
Parrawe
Heka
Warringa
HELLYER GORGE STATE RESERVE
Companion Hill
Lower Wilmot
Saint Valentines Peak
Upper Castra
Barrington
Nook
Railton
Murchison
Loongana Range
Nietta
Merseylea
Mount Everett
Sheffield
Magnet Range
Belmont Hill
Gatcomb Plain
Narrawa
Wilmot
West Kentish
Stoodley
Kimberley
Mount Bischoff
South Nietta
Roland
Two Hummocks
Mount Tor
Promised Land
Paradise
Waratah
Guildford
Black Bluff
Beulah
Mount Cleveland
A10
Erriba
Staverton
Weegena
Lower Beulah
BLACK BLUFF NATURE RECREATION AREA
Moina
Gowrie Park
Cethana
Mount Vandyke
Dunorlan
B23
Mount Pearse
Mount Cattley
Moory Mount
Stormont
Mount Claude
Gog Range
Magog
Prospect Mountain
Mole Creek
Netherby Plain
Lorinna
Daisy Dell
Liena
Chudleigh
Mount Ramsay
Mount Cripps
Middlesex Plains
Mayberry
Marakoopa Cave
Emu Plains
Caveside
Joins Map 3
Joins Map 6
Highway
Bass
Road
Mount
River
Forth
Mersey
Leven

Joins Map 2
N
0
50km
BASS STRAIT
Crop Poi
WATERHOU CONSERVAT AREA
West Sandy Point
East Sandy Point
Anderson Bay
Granite Point
Jerusalem Plains
Stony Head
Lulworth
Fordington
Bridport
Five Mile Bluff
Beechford
Weymouth
Bellingham
Back Creek
B82
West Head
Low Head
George Town
Badger Head
Greens Beach
Kelso
Clarence Point
Point Sorell
Hawley Beach
Lefroy
Pipers River
Pipers Brook
Little Ballroom
Badger Hill
North Scottsda
Jetsonville
Scottsd
Tippogoree Hills
East Tamar
NARAWNTAPU NATIONAL PARK
Shearwater
Northdown
Port Sorell
Dazzler Range
Ilfraville
Beauty Point
Rowella
Kayena
The Glen
Lower Turners Marsh
Lebrina
Golconda
Wyena
Blumont
Greeta
Lietinna
West Scottsdale
Tongana Cuckoo
Wesley Vale
Thirlstane
Moriarty
Harford
Beaconsfield
West Tamar
Sidmouth
Deviot
Hillwood
Mount Direction
Highway
Tunnel
Lisle
Springfield
South Springfiel
Sassafras
Bass
B71
Holwell
Winkleigh
Bald Tier
A7
Gravelly Beach
A8
Turners Marsh
Lilydale
Mount Arthur
Myrtle Bank
A3
Weelaty
The Sideling
Mount Scott
Exeter
Lanena
Underwood
Targa
Stony Rises
Frankford
Glengarry
Dilston
Patersonia
Tasman
Diddleum Plains
Grindelwald
Tamar
Mount Barrow
Tayena
Mersey Lea
Sunnyside
Kimberley
Parkham
Black Sugarloaf
Bridgenorth
Legana
Rocherlea
Splitters Tier
Nunamara
South Barrow
Birralee
Hut Tier
Rosevale
Stephens Hill
Ravenswood
Waverley
1
Reedy Marsh
Launceston
Burns Creek
Upper Blessington
Moltema
Elizabeth Town
Weegena
Weetah
Selbourne
Norwood
Shoulder of Mutton Plain
Midland
Dunorlan
Westwood
Corra Linn
Hadspen
Relbia
Kangaroo Hills
Bengeo
Highway
Exton
Deloraine
Westbury
Hagley
Carrick
Breadalbane
Blessington
Western Junction
Pateena
Chudleigh
Needles
Osmaston
Glenore
Perth
Evandale
Whitemore
Quamby Brook
Cluan
Montana
Toiberry
Longford
Deddington
Joins Map 7
A
B
C
D
E
F
1
2
3
4
5
6
7
8

TOURING MAPS

Joins Map 1
A
B
C
D
E
F
1
2
3
4
5
6
7
8
Mount Sunday
Badger Plains
Savage River
Longback
ARTHUR-PIEMAN CONSERVATION AREA
West Plain
Mount Donaldson
Meredith Range
Rupert Point
Pieman
Corinna
Mount Livingstone
Pieman Head
Bernafai Ridge
Conical Rocks Point
Yarrana Hill
Reece Dam
Ahrberg Bay
Granville Harbour
Mount Heemskirk
MOUNT HEEMSKIRK REGIONAL RESERVE
Mount Agnew
Trial Harbour
Henty Dunes
Ocean Beach
SOUTHERN OCEAN
Hells Gates
Macquarie Heads
Sloop Point
Gorge Point
Birthday Bay
Varna Bay
Hibbs Bay
Point Hibbs
N
0
50km
Joins Map 9

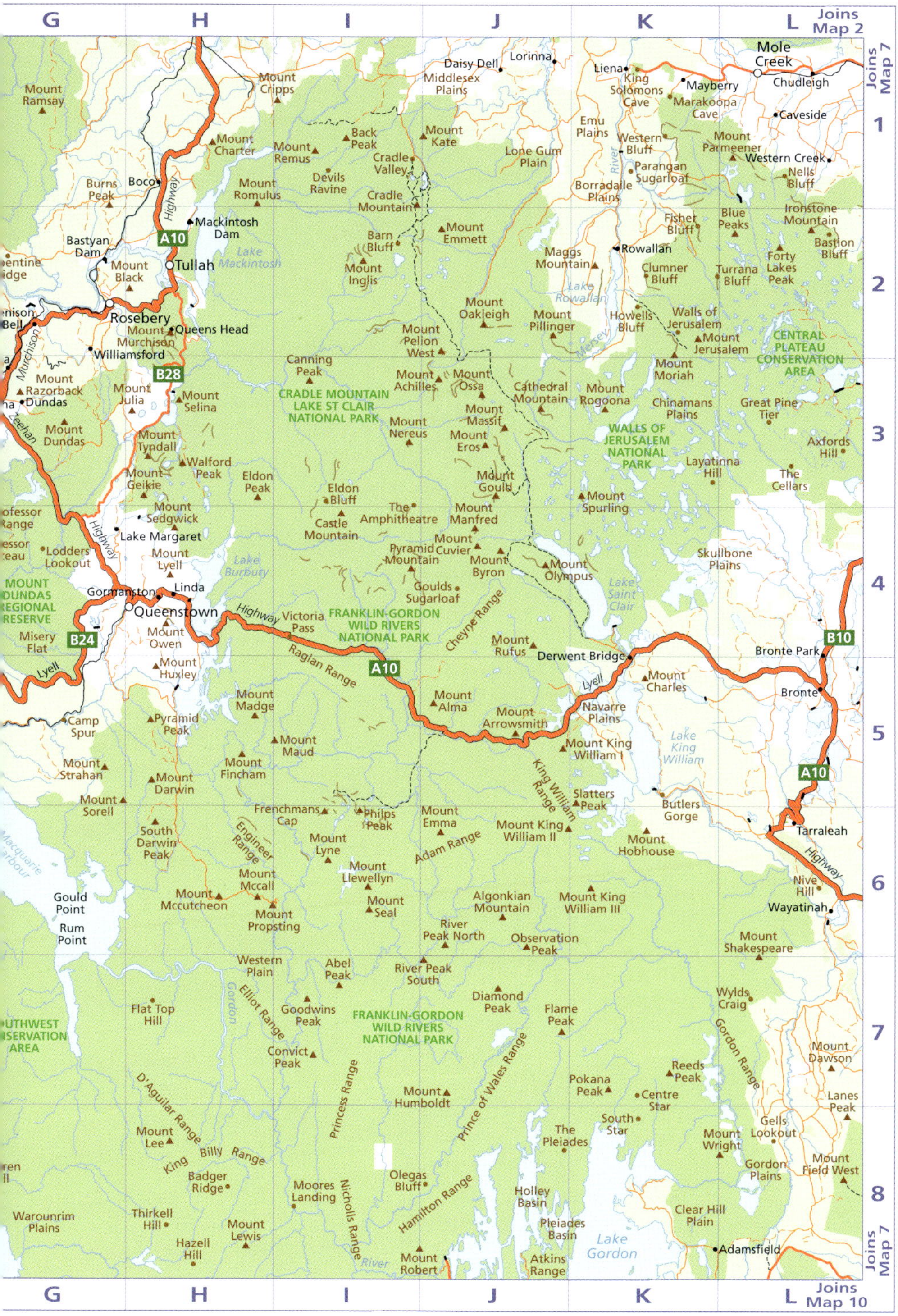
G
H
I
J
K
L
Joins Map 2
Joins Map 7
Joins Map 10
1
2
3
4
5
6
7
8
Mount Ramsay
Mount Cripps
Daisy Dell
Lorinna
Middlesex Plains
Liena
King Solomons Cave
Mayberry
Marakoopa Cave
Mole Creek
Chudleigh
Caveside
Mount Charter
Mount Remus
Back Peak
Mount Kate
Emu Plains
Western Bluff
Mount Parmeener
Western Creek
Nells Bluff
Cradle Valley
Lone Gum Plain
Parangan Sugarloaf
Burns Peak
Boco
Mount Romulus
Devils Ravine
Cradle Mountain
Borradaile Plains
River
Highway
Mackintosh Dam
Fisher Bluff
Blue Peaks
Ironstone Mountain
Bastyan Dam
A10
Barn Bluff
Mount Emmett
Rowallan
Bastion Bluff
Lake Mackintosh
Maggs Mountain
Forty Lakes Peak
Mount Black
Tullah
Mount Inglis
Clumner Bluff
Turrana Bluff
Lake Rowallan
Rosebery
Mount Oakleigh
Mount Pillinger
Howells Bluff
Walls of Jerusalem
Mount Murchison
Queens Head
Mount Pelion West
Mount Jerusalem
Murchison
Williamsford
Mersey
CENTRAL PLATEAU CONSERVATION AREA
Canning Peak
Mount Achilles
Mount Ossa
Mount Moriah
Mount Razorback
B28
Cathedral Mountain
Mount Rogoona
Dundas
Mount Julia
Mount Selina
CRADLE MOUNTAIN LAKE ST CLAIR NATIONAL PARK
Mount Massif
Chinamans Plains
Great Pine Tier
Mount Dundas
Zeehan
Mount Nereus
Mount Eros
WALLS OF JERUSALEM NATIONAL PARK
Axfords Hill
Mount Tyndall
Walford Peak
Eldon Peak
Layatinna Hill
Mount Geikie
Mount Gould
The Cellars
Eldon Bluff
Mount Spurling
Mount Sedgwick
The Amphitheatre
Mount Manfred
Castle Mountain
Lake Margaret
Lodders Lookout
Mount Cuvier
Pyramid Mountain
Skullbone Plains
Mount Lyell
Lake Burbury
Mount Byron
Mount Olympus
MOUNT DUNDAS REGIONAL RESERVE
Linda
Gormanston
Goulds Sugarloaf
Lake Saint Clair
Queenstown
Victoria Pass
FRANKLIN-GORDON WILD RIVERS NATIONAL PARK
Cheyne Range
Mount Owen
Misery Flat
B24
Mount Rufus
Derwent Bridge
Bronte Park
B10
Raglan Range
Mount Huxley
Lyell
Mount Charles
Bronte
Mount Madge
Mount Alma
Navarre Plains
Camp Spur
Pyramid Peak
Mount Arrowsmith
Mount Maud
Mount King William I
Lake King William
Mount Strahan
Mount Fincham
King William Range
Mount Darwin
Slatters Peak
Mount Sorell
Frenchmans Cap
Philps Peak
Mount Emma
Butlers Gorge
Tarraleah
Engineer Range
Mount King William II
South Darwin Peak
Mount Lyne
Adam Range
Mount Hobhouse
Macquarie Harbour
Mount Llewellyn
Mount Mccall
Nive Hill
Gould Point
Mount Mccutcheon
Algonkian Mountain
Mount King William III
Wayatinah
Mount Seal
Mount Propsting
Rum Point
River Peak North
Observation Peak
Mount Shakespeare
Western Plain
Abel Peak
River Peak South
Diamond Peak
Wylds Craig
Flat Top Hill
Goodwins Peak
Flame Peak
Gordon
Elliot Range
FRANKLIN-GORDON WILD RIVERS NATIONAL PARK
Gordon Range
Convict Peak
Mount Dawson
Reeds Peak
Pokana Peak
Mount Humboldt
Centre Star
Lanes Peak
D'Aguilar Range
Princess Range
Prince of Wales Range
South Star
Gells Lookout
Mount Lee
The Pleiades
Mount Wright
Billy Range
King
Gordon Plains
Mount Field West
Badger Ridge
Olegas Bluff
Moores Landing
Nicholls Range
Hamilton Range
Holley Basin
Clear Hill Plain
Warounrim Plains
Thirkell Hill
Mount Lewis
Pleiades Basin
Hazell Hill
Lake Gordon
Adamsfield
River
Mount Robert
Atkins Range

Joins Map 3
A
B
C
D
E
F
Joins Map 6
1
2
3
4
5
6
7
8
Westbury
Hagley
Carrick
Breadalbane
Blessington
Chudleigh
Needles
Pateena
Western Junction
Perth
Evandale
Lowes Mount
Caveside
Montana
Quamby Brook
Glenore
Cluan
Whitemore
Longford
Deddington
Stockers Plains
Golden Valley
Bishopsbourne
Toiberry
Clarendon
Western Creek
Meander
Cobblers Hill
Bracknell
B51
Nile
Lake
Liffey
Cressy
B53
Powranna
Drys Bluff
Great Western Tiers
Liffey Bluff
Midland
1
Ironstone Mountain
Projection Bluff
Blackwood Creek
South
Massey Hill
Johnstones Peak
A5
Cathcart Bluff
Epping Forest
Highway
Breona
Poatina
Marquarie
Cleveland
CENTRAL PLATEAU CONSERVATION AREA
Brandum
Mount Blackwood
Llewellyn
Lake Augusta
Conara
Bernacchi
GREAT LAKE CONSERVATION AREA
O'Connors Peak
Reynolds Neck
Isis
Cramps Bay
Mount Kingstone
Great Western Tiers
Liawenee
Great Lake
B51
The Cellars
Campbell Town
Skittleball Hill
Tods Corner
Saddle Hill
Miena
Mount Patrick
Wild Hops Hill
GREAT WESTERN TIERS CONSERVATION AREA
Burburys Sugarloaf
Mount Augusta
Flintstone
Arthurs Lake
Highway
The Springs
Barren Tier
Handsome Flat
B11
Wilburville
Ross
Woods Lake
Mount Penny
Smiths Tops
Shannon
Mount Franklin
Marlborough
River
Nive
Gavins Tier
1
Mona Vale
Lake Sorell
Steppes
Hilltop
Bakers Tier
Silver Plains
Highway
Bronte Park
Waddamana
Diamond Tier
London Lakes
Lake Echo
Tunbridge Tier
Tunbridge
Interlaken
Bashan Ledge
Lake
Shannon Tier
Clyde
Lake Crescent
Woodbury
Mount Serat
River
Antill Ponds
Black Tier
Front Tier
Carrot Hill
A5
A10
Table Mountain
Mount Pleasant
Hermitage
Dee
York Plains
Native Tier
Pawtella
Cluny Hill
Oatlands
Tarraleah
Little Blue Hill
Halfmoon Tier
Lagoon Hill
Mount Anstey
Victoria Valley
Andover
Lyell
Osterley
Nicholas Sugarloaf
Lower Marshes
Midland
Parattah
Ouse
Black Bobs
Mount Seymour
Mount Burrows
Strickland
Bothwell
Green Hill
Jericho
Wayatinah
Highway
Stonor
Mount Seymour
Spring Hill Tier
River
Den Hill
Baden
Whitefoo
Apsley
Mount Reid
Mour Ponsor
Stony Peak
Lake Tiberias
Broncos Hill
Tunnack
Woodsdale
River
Mount Mercer
Mount Thunderbolt
Ouse
Black Tier
Melton Mowbray
Rhyndaston
Midland
Mount Hobbs
Mount Clark
Mount Dawson
Lawrenny
Kempton
Hollow Tree
Colebrook
A10
Mount Bains
Hamilton
1
Petham Tier
Sendace Hills
Abbotts Hill
Brown Mountain
Dysart
Bullock Hills
Mount Lord
Derwent
Highway
Brown Mountain
Mount Field West
Ellendale
Mount Bethune
Elderslie
Rodway Range
Bagdad
Highway
Runnymede
Fentonbury
Mount Fenton
Broadmarsh
Mangalore
Campania
Westerway
Platform Peak
Gretna
Mour Phipp
MOUNT FIELD NATIONAL PARK
National Park
Pontville
Mount Dromedary
Tea Tree
Rosegarland
Brighton
Bushy Park
Black Hills
Tyenne
Conlans Hill
Bridgewater
Richmond
Pawle
Plenty
Dromedary
Orielton
Fitzgerald
Joins Map 11

G
H
I
J
K
L
Joins Map 4
1
2
3
4
5
6
7
8
Joins Map 12
Ben Lomond
Tower Hill
Dublin Town
Mount Nicholas
Mount Durham
Cornwall
Four Mile Creek
Ironhouse Point
Blackboy Ridge
St Marys
Mangana
Mount Elephant
Wardlaws Point
Break O'Day Plains
Gray
Bare Rock
Gray Hills
Storys Creek
Sawpit Ridge
Mount Clara
Fingal
Rossarden
Mount Malcolm
Mount Edgecombe
Dogwood Hill
Chain of Lagoons
Piccaninny Point
Highway
CASTLE CARY REGIONAL RESERVE
River
A4
Fingal Tier
A3
Castle Cary
Mount Foster
Mount Puzzler
Mount Punter
Lookout Hill
Seymour
St Pauls Dome
Mount Slaughter
Mount St John
DOUGLAS-APSLEY NATIONAL PARK
Douglas River
Avoca
Mount St Peter
Pennefathers Knob
Mount Allen
Royal George
Mount Henry
Mount Andrew
Lewis Hill
Bicheno
Campbell Town
Lynes Sugarloaf
Snow Hill
Tasman
Tar Hill
Cape Lodi
Teatree Hill
Ferrars Tier
Butlers Point
Rogers Hill
Island Hill
B34
Lake Leake
Cranbrook
Mount Peter
Moulting Lagoon
Mount Morriston
Mount Paul
Friendly Point
Eagle Ridge
FREYCINET NATIONAL PARK
A3
Swansea
Little Blue Tier
Coles Bay
Cape Tourville
Gentle Annie
Mount Dove
Webber Point
Skippys Tier
Great Oyster Bay
Cape Forestier
Stoneyard Hill
Mount Tooms
Mount Freycinet
Shelly Point
Weatherhead Point
Mount Lofty
Green Tier
Freycinet Peninsula
Cape Degerando
Boags Point
Schouten Passage
Marshalls Tier
Royalty Ridge
Little Swanport
Highway
Seaford Point
Schouten Island
Cape Faure
Cape Sonnerat
Point Bailly
Ravensdale
Mount Murray
TASMAN SEA
Mount Douglas
Triabunna
Cape Bougainville
Louisville
Orford
Cape Boullanger
A3
Tasman
Buckland
Spring Beach
Darlington
Mount Maria
Rheban
Loafers Hill
Mercury Passage
Mount Calvary
MARIA ISLAND NATIONAL PARK
Mistaken Cape
Little Raggedy Head
Nugent
Mount Walter
Cape Peron
N
0
50km

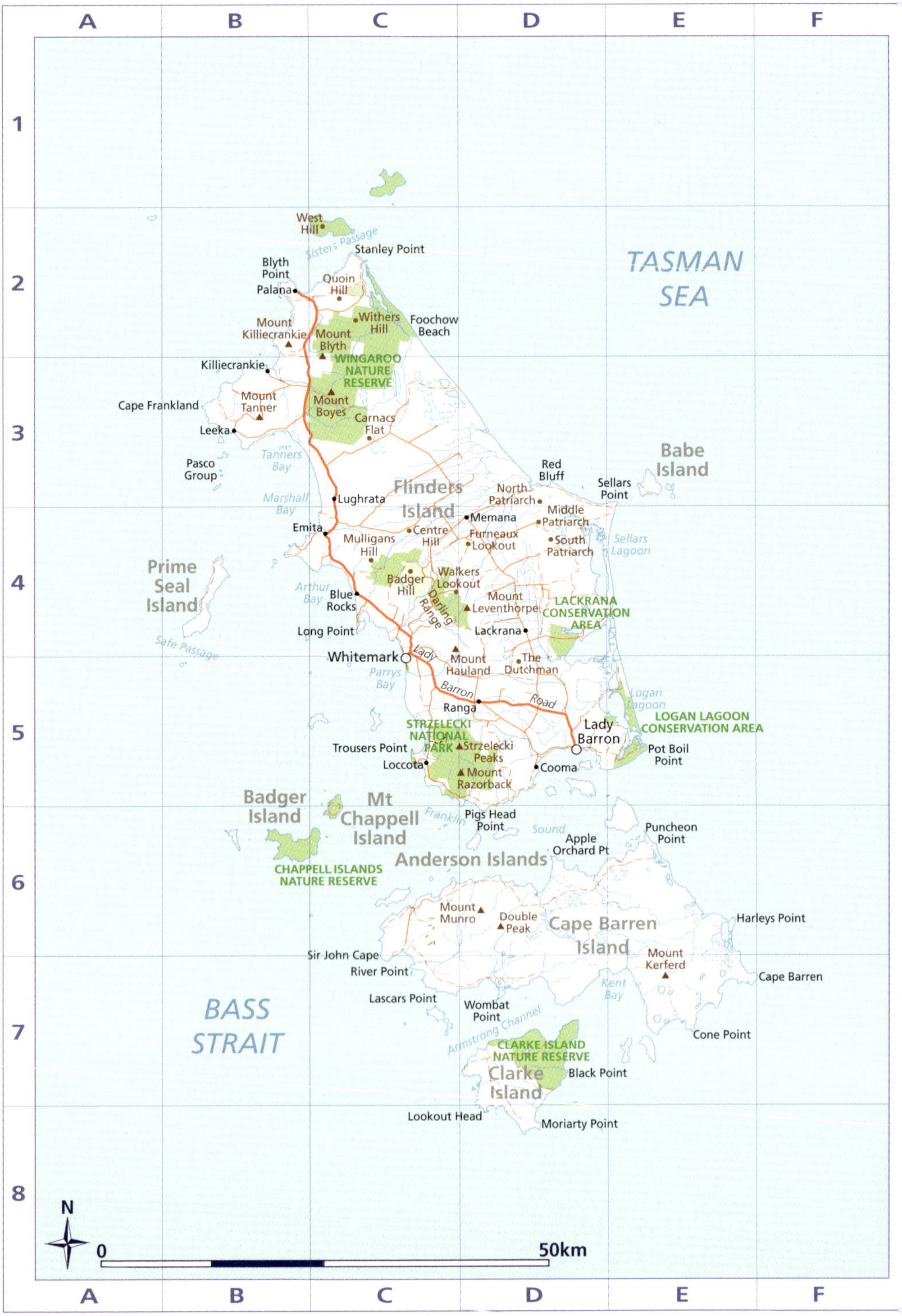
A
B
C
D
E
F
1
2
3
4
5
6
7
8
TASMAN SEA
BASS STRAIT
West Hill
Sisters Passage
Stanley Point
Blyth Point
Palana
Quoin Hill
Withers Hill
Foochow Beach
Mount Killiecrankie
Mount Blyth
WINGAROO NATURE RESERVE
Killiecrankie
Mount Tanner
Mount Boyes
Cape Frankland
Carnacs Flat
Leeka
Tanners Bay
Pasco Group
Marshall Bay
Lughrata
Flinders Island
Red Bluff
North Patriarch
Sellars Point
Babe Island
Memana
Middle Patriarch
Emita
Centre Hill
Furneaux Lookout
South Patriarch
Sellars Lagoon
Mulligans Hill
Badger Hill
Walkers Lookout
Prime Seal Island
Arthur Bay
Blue Rocks
Darling Range
Mount Leventhorpe
LACKRANA CONSERVATION AREA
Long Point
Lackrana
Safe Passage
Whitemark
Lady Barron Road
Mount Hauland
The Dutchman
Parrys Bay
Ranga
Logan Lagoon
LOGAN LAGOON CONSERVATION AREA
Lady Barron
STRZELECKI NATIONAL PARK
Strzelecki Peaks
Trousers Point
Pot Boil Point
Loccota
Cooma
Mount Razorback
Badger Island
Mt Chappell Island
Franklin Sound
Pigs Head Point
Puncheon Point
Apple Orchard Pt
Anderson Islands
CHAPPELL ISLANDS NATURE RESERVE
Mount Munro
Double Peak
Cape Barren Island
Harleys Point
Sir John Cape
River Point
Mount Kerferd
Cape Barren
Kent Bay
Lascars Point
Wombat Point
Armstrong Channel
Cone Point
CLARKE ISLAND NATURE RESERVE
Clarke Island
Black Point
Lookout Head
Moriarty Point
N
0
50km

TOURING MAPS

Joins Map 7
Joins Map 10
A
B
C
D
E
F
1
2
3
4
5
6
7
8
Westerway
National Park
Gretna
Rosegarland
Pontville
Brighton
Tea Tree
Brains Hill
A3
Pawle
Junee Cave
Tyenne
Bushy Park
Lyell Highway
A10
Dromedary
Bridgewater
Richmond
Orielton
The Needles
Fitzgerald
Maydena
Plenty
Hayes
Magra
Boyer
Granton
Gagebrook
Mount Lord
Sor
Mount Mueller
Maynes Hill
Risbys Plains
Abbotts Lookout
Uxbridge
Moogara
New Norfolk
Malbina
1
Old Beach
Claremont
Berriedale
Otago
Dulcot
Penna
Midway Point
Highway
River
Holness Hill
Blue Gum Knob
Lachlan
Collinsvale
Glenorchy
Cambridge
Lindisfarne
Seven Mile Beach
Lewishar
Dodg Ferry
Snowy North
Mount Styx
Mount Jubilee
Tasman
HOBART
Howrah
Rokeby
Frederick Henry Bay
Wetpants Peak
Snowy Range
Mount Jackson
Fern Tree
Derwent
North East Ridge
Mountain River
Ridgeway
Sandy Bay
Lauderdale
Russell Ridge
Neika
Sandford
Snowy South
Lonnavale
Mount Misery
Crabtree
Longley
Highway
Taroona
Cremo
SOUTHWEST NATIONAL PARK
Grove
A6
Kingston
Mount Sarah Jane
Lucaston
Lower Longley
Sandfly
Clifton Beach
Judbury
Blackmans Bay
Opossum Bay
Bernard Spur
Ranelagh
Kaoota
Margate
Mount Weld
River
Glen Huon
Lanes Hill
Huonville
Howden
South Arm
Electrona
Tinderbox
Mount Frederick
Arve Plains
Snug
Dennes Point
Outer No Head
Woodstock
Coningham
Franklin
Huon
Cradoc
Oyster Cove
Castle Forbes Bay
Fourfoot Plain
Galleries Hill
Kettering
Barnes Bay
Mount Riveaux
Woodbridge Hill
B68
Storm Bay
Port Huon
Cygnet
The Razorback
Mount Picton
Geeveston
Woodbridge
Gardners Bay
Cairns Bay
Birchs Bay
Mount Chapman
Devils Backbone
Lymington
Flowerpot
Channel
Church Hill
Waterloo
Garden Island Creek
Mount Hopetoun
Burgess Bluff
Surges Bay
Highway
Middleton
Hartz Peak
Glendevie
Police Point
Hartz Mountains
Verona Sands
Isthmus Bay
Cape Queen Elizabeth
Gordon
A6
Federation Peak
Surveyors Bay
Simpsons Bay
Walpole
Glenbervie
Mount Bobs
New
Esperance Peak
Dover
Alonnah
Adventure Bay
Raminea
Ventenat Point
Strathblane
Adamsons Peak
Mount Bounty
Adventure Bay
SOUTHWEST NATIONAL PARK
Tylers Hill
Lomas Hill
Lunawanna
Huon
River
Great Taylors Bay
Bruny Island
Cape Connella
Mount Alexandra
Hays Hill
Mount Bleak
Lune River
Southport
Mount Bisdee
Ida Bay
Cloudy Bay
Mangana Bluff
Precipitous Bluff
Mount Victoria Cross
Mount Bruny
Mount Barren
Ironbound Range
East Cloudy Head
Mount La Perouse
Cape Bruny
Boreel Head
Pindars Peak
Tasman Head
Eliza Point
Havelock Bluff
Prion Bay
South Cape Range
Cockle Creek
Shoemaker Point
Bare Hill
South Cape Bay
South Cape
Whale Head
South East Cape
N
0
50km

G
H
I
J
K
L
Joins Map 8
1
2
3
4
5
6
7
8
Ringrove Razorback
Nugent
eans Hill
Mount Reuben
Cape Bernier
Cape Maurouard
Cape Peron
Iles Tier
Kellevie
Marion Bay
ett
Arthur
Bream Creek
Copping
Cape Paul Lamanon
Cape Frederick Hendrick
Primrose Sands
Dunalley
Mount Reynolds
A9
Forestier Peninsula
High Yellow Bluff
Whitehouse Point
Murdunna
Highway
View Peak
Cape Surville
ount ewart
Norfolk Bay
Macgregor Peak
Eaglehawk Neck
Saltwater River
Premaydena
Taranna
Koonya
Clemes Peak
O'Hara Bluff
ubeena
Thumbs Point
White each
Tasman Peninsula
Dolomieu Point
Cape Hauy
Highcroft
Port Arthur
Mount Fortescue
Stormlea
Mount Raoul
Munro Bight
alters Point
Maingon Bay
Cape Pillar
Cape Raoul
ASMAN SEA

Port Davey Walking Track, Southwest National Park

Parks, Forests, Reserves and Campsites Index

M

N

O

P

R

S

***Denotes areas with facilities (usually special access to toilets) for people with disabilities**

Lake St Clair - Lake St Clair Tourist Park

Campsite Index

*** Denotes areas with facilities (usually special access to toilets) for people with disabilities**

Tahune Air Walk, Southern Forests

Boiling Billy and

The Camping Guide to Tasmania is just one of a growing series of outdoor and souvenir guides from Boiling Billy and co-publishers Woodslane Press.

Boiling Billy have been publishing guides for the Australian outdoor enthusiast for over 20 years, and details of all their titles can be found at www.boilingbilly.com.au They are now co-publishing with Woodslane Press, one of Australia's leading book distributors and publishers. To browse through other titles available from Woodslane Press, visit www.woodslane.com.au If your local bookshop does not have stock of a Boiling Billy or Woodslane Press book, they can easily order it for you. In case of difficulty please contact our customer service team on 02 8445 2300 or info@woodslane.com.au

Camping Guide to NSW 5/e
$34.99
ISBN: 9781921203688

Camping Guide to Victoria 5/e
$34.99
ISBN: 9781925403381

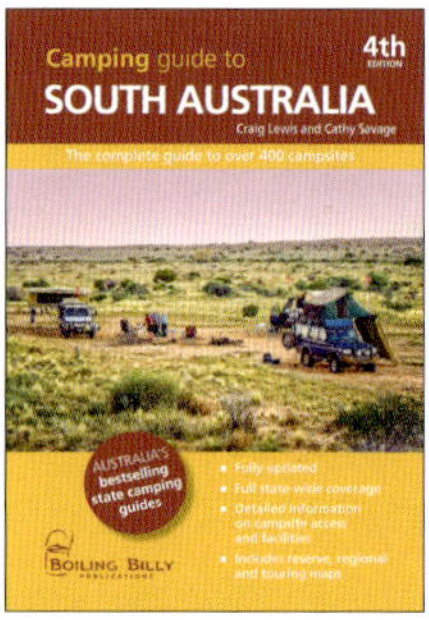

Camping Guide to South Australia 4/e
$34.99
ISBN: 9781925403862

Camping Guide to Western Australia 3/e
$34.99
ISBN: 9781921606168

Camping Guide to Queensland 5/e
$34.99
ISBN: 9781925403954

Camping Guide to the Northern Territory 4/e
$29.99
ISBN: 9781925403879

Australian Bush Cooking 3/e
$34.99
ISBN: 9781921203930

Australian Camp Oven Cooking
$34.99
ISBN: 9781921874901

Woodslane Press

Hobart's Best Bush, Coast & City Walks

$29.99

ISBN: 9781921683664

Best Bush, Coast and Village Walks of South East Tasmania

$34.99

ISBN: 9781922131195

Australian Geographic: Tasmania

$19.99

ISBN: 9781925403923

Australian Bush Pubs 2/e

$49.99

ISBN: 9781925403411

High Country Huts & Homesteads

$49.99

ISBN: 9781925403398

Where to Ride Tasmania 2/e

$34.99

ISBN: 9781921874307

Walkers on the Overland Track,
Cradle Mt - Lake St Clair National Park